Books like *Befriend* have me hopeful that God's people are going to rise to the occasion of our moment in history with God's goodness and grace. I pray that as you read through each of these chapters, you might add more serious and diverse friendships to enrich and expand your view of what God is up to in our day. I couldn't be more grateful for Scott's voice on this topic.

MATT CHANDLER
Pastor of The Village Church, author of *The Explicit Gospel*, and coauthor of *The Mingling of Souls*

Scott Sauls is a pastor even through his writing. He doesn't preach; he cares for souls and gently reminds us of a better way, of the tension and beauty of following Jesus. Jesus was and is a friend. Scott not only writes masterfully about that but lives like Jesus in this way.

JENNIE ALLEN
Founder/visionary of IF:Gathering and author of *Anything* and *Restless*

In this accessible book, Scott Sauls looks at virtually the entirety of the Christian life through the prism of friendship, and that's a well-grounded project theologically. When the gospel makes God our friend rather than our enemy, and we are also reconciled to ourselves—both our sin and our identity in Jesus, our friend—then we move out into the world in a new way. As Scott so ably shows us, Christian practice is to a great degree an exercise in friendship. This is a helpful, practical, and rich encouragement to bring all of our life in line with the gospel.

TIMOTHY KELLER
Senior pastor of Redeemer Presbyterian Church in New York City

In *Befriend*, Scott Sauls provides *real* rescue from loneliness by highlighting what it means to be in real relationship and exposing the difference between "friending" and "befriending." In a world full of "likes," Scott points us back to *love*. There could not be a better time for a book such as this one.

ELISABETH HASSELBECK
Talk show host, wife and mother, and author of *The G-Free Diet*

It feels ironic that in an age when connectivity is on the rise, so is loneliness. Friendships, real friendships, aren't always easy, but they are always important. I'm glad that Scott has taken such an honest look at something we all need more of. And because he's my friend, he forgave me for ending that last sentence with a preposition and beginning this one with *and*.

JON ACUFF
New York Times bestselling author of *Do Over*

Simply stated, this book is important. For the kind of humans we want to be in the world in which we are living, *Befriend* is what we need to read and use as a guidebook as we work hard to love our neighbors well. Wanting to be culture shapers requires effort and focus, and Scott pastors us all toward that end in this and all of his writings. I'm grateful for his voice in my life and in our culture.

ANNIE DOWNS
Bestselling author of *Looking for Lovely* and *Let's All Be Brave*

One of the major problems facing people today is loneliness. Friendships are hard to form and even harder to maintain. Isolation and superficiality are easier but deaden the soul. Respected pastor Scott Sauls here presents a Christian vision of deep friendship. This book is wise, biblical, and practical. It could help change your life.

RUSSELL MOORE
President, Southern Baptist Ethics & Religious Liberty Commission

Today's Christians have a reputation for shaking our fists at our culture rather than shining a light within it. What if instead we led with 1 Corinthians 13 love, risking relationships with those we might otherwise avoid—locally and across the globe? That's what Scott Sauls challenges us to do in *Befriend*. This timely book is a guide for you and me to address relationship barriers we may not even be aware of and courageously engage heart-first in our world, drawing closer to Jesus as we do.

RICH STEARNS
President/CEO of World Vision

We Christians know that love is the "greatest of these," yet we struggle to live out that love alongside other loved sinners. In this highly readable and timely book, pastor Scott Sauls draws on Scripture, pop culture, and his own life to illuminate the various and often unlikely people we are called to love. I hope and pray that this book will give more of us a deeper knowledge of our own belovedness in Christ, a knowledge that can set us free to love others well and with abandon.

KATELYN BEATY
Print managing editor, *Christianity Today* magazine,
and author of *A Woman's Place*

When I turned forty, I made myself a promise—to throw myself into a resource I had long neglected while frantically climbing Mount Significance—people and friendships. While I've made significant headway, my only regrets are that I didn't do this sooner, and that I didn't have my friend Scott Sauls' book *Befriend* as a treasure trove to guide me on the journey. *Befriend* is a book I will return to time and again . . . with friends, to both learn and be inspired in experiencing both the deepest longing and greatest challenge of my heart—true friendship.

BRYAN LORITTS
Lead pastor of Abundant Life Church and author of *Saving the Saved*

Scott teaches us about befriending others by showing us how graciously Jesus has first befriended us. *Befriend* is both wise and earthy, relevant and practical. But most of all, as Scott reveals his own need for Jesus, amid the very real questions of our generation, we too see our own need and our own questions. This leaves all of us looking to Jesus. Thank you, Scott.

ZACK ESWINE
Pastor of Riverside Church and author of *The Imperfect Pastor*

As Scott Sauls says in *Befriend*, "Real friendship happens when we move *toward* the people we are most tempted to avoid." Sauls challenges us to break free of those things than hinder us from befriending others, not by our own strength and might, but by the power of God through love. If God so loved the world, shouldn't we? *Befriend* helps us embrace this awesome calling and moves us one step closer to one another.

TRILLIA NEWBELL
Author of *Enjoy* (forthcoming 2017), *Fear and Faith*, and *United*

In an age of isolation, loneliness, and social fragmentation, there is a tremendous opportunity for the church to offer what Jesus offers: deep community to those who need it, namely all of humanity. With disarming candor and gritty realism, Scott Sauls demonstrates how to apply the gospel to befriend a wide range of broken image bearers . . . a group that includes you and me. A life-giving read for such a time as this.

BRIAN FIKKERT
Coauthor of *When Helping Hurts: How to Alleviate Poverty without Hurting the Poor . . . and Yourself*

In a world of superficial acquaintances, Scott Sauls casts a compelling vision of a better way. In *Befriend*, he insightfully diagnoses what's missing in our relationships and prescribes a practical and hopeful way forward. This book will challenge your assumptions of what friendships are with a fresh view of what they could be. Read this book with caution; it will move, convict, and stretch you to experience the kind of friendships God intended.

DARREN WHITEHEAD
Pastor, Church of the City, Nashville, and author of *Rumors of God*

Scott Sauls is the real deal! Honest, vulnerable, funny . . . In *Befriend* he teaches us how to lose control in order to find a better way—a way full of freedom, joy, intimate community, safe harbor, and warm hospitality for those who often live on the margins of the church and society by no fault of their own—the Way of Jesus. I hope you'll read the book and take it to heart!

JEREMY COURTNEY
CEO and president of Preemptive Love Coalition

Befriend is a book about the everyday work of being a neighbor. It is as practical as it is pastoral, inviting us to bridge indifference, suspicion, even hostility to love the world God so loved. Sauls writes with refreshing humility and biblical wisdom: his is a voice to trust.

JEN POLLOCK MICHEL
Award-winning author of *Teach Us to Want* and *Keeping Place*

Befriend is a practical, winsome, and engaging book that explores the complexities of friendship in ways that are bound to make you uncomfortable and to inspire you to look at your friends anew. Grounded in theology and personal experience, Scott Sauls's book is a great daily devotional, small group study, or personal study on friendship and the gospel.

ALAN NOBLE
Editor in chief of *Christ and Pop Culture* and assistant professor of English, Oklahoma Baptist University

I've never seen Scott Sauls back down from a difficult topic. And I've never seen him miss an opportunity to make much of God's grace abounding in Jesus. In our age of judgment, isolation, and fear Scott shows us what a friend we have in Jesus.

COLLIN HANSEN
Editorial director of The Gospel Coalition and author of *Blind Spots: Becoming a Courageous, Compassionate, and Commissioned Church*

Befriend calls us to something beautiful, something important, something better. In an age where engaging, complex relationships are so easily passed over for effortless, superficial counterfeits, Scott Sauls calls us from the shadows of pretending into the light of real friendship. Anyone who has ever felt even the slightest emotional reaction to how they fare in the world of social media will find in this book a reasoned path to the truth about who we are and how we were made to relate to one another. I am so thankful for my friend Scott Sauls's wisdom, courage, and voice.

RUSS RAMSEY
Pastor, author of *Behold the King of Glory*, and content editor for *She/He Reads Truth*

I simply wasn't prepared for the power, impact, and deeply convicting thoughts included in *Befriend* by Scott Sauls. But the reality is that many of the most convicting words were spoken by Jesus before they were repeated by Scott. The scandalous and profound truth is that not only did Jesus speak these words, he lived them. This is where *Befriend* shines the focused spotlight. Steadfast in truth, agile in love. Like I said, I wasn't prepared, but I am propelled by what happened in my soul through this beautiful work of words.

DAN WOLGEMUTH
President/CEO of Youth for Christ USA

I'll be honest. This book scares me. Jesus said the heart of our life with God and others is relationship, but so many of us—me included—rarely come close to plumbing the depths of what true relationship is. Real love is terrifying. True intimacy makes you so . . . vulnerable. And selflessness is a kind of dying. In *Befriend*, Scott Sauls takes us on an emotional, honest, and at times raw journey we all need to take.

CAREY NIEUWHOF
Host of the *Carey Nieuwhof Leadership Podcast*, author, and founding pastor of Connexus Church

In an increasingly fractious age in which we reduce each other to soundbites, demographics, and stereotypes, burying ourselves deeper in social media silos with those who think like us, Scott Sauls gently and prophetically reminds us of the power of befriending those who are different, reminding of Jesus' habit of seeing the image of God in the "other." This is an urgent and healing book.

MARK SAYERS
Senior pastor of Red Church in Melbourne, Australia, and author of *Facing Leviathan* and *Disappearing Church*

How can we begin to heal the wounds of division that plague our polarized society? It won't happen with another think piece or hot-take blog rant. No amount of tweeting or texting will solve it. It will only happen in the context of real, flesh-and-blood relationships. This is why Scott Sauls's simple yet profound book *Befriend* is so valuable and timely. From a variety of angles and with a wide array of stories and examples, Sauls cuts through the partisan clutter and makes a compelling case for friendship as a way to break the stalemate.

BRETT MCCRACKEN
Author of *Hipster Christianity* and *Gray Matters*

Scott Sauls understands a vital truth and writes about it with refreshingly accessible but persistently gracious challenge: the gospel comes alive for us more through the risk of relationships than through assent to theological precepts and moral teachings. Making ourselves vulnerably present to others in genuine friendship is God's way of taking on flesh and blood among us. After all, this was the way of Jesus. In today's cultural environment tenuously held together by thin lines of social connection, *Befriend* offers faithful encouragement and wisdom on the importance of genuine friendship, thankfully perhaps not yet a lost calling for the church.

THE REV. R. LEIGH SPRUILL
Rector, St. George's Church, Nashville, Tennessee

Christ's people must avoid two sacrifices: love on the altar of truth, and truth on the altar of love. Scott Sauls's voice is a refreshing alternative to the bombast that fills our airwaves and, sadly, many of our pulpits. With keen insight and elegant prose, Scott shows us how to engage our world in a winsome yet subversive manner.

MATT SMETHURST
Managing editor of The Gospel Coalition

We live in the most connected generation in history, and yet we may be the most disconnected generation in history. My friend Scott Sauls calls Christians to something deeper, to be intentional about friendship in a way that is a catalyst for change. This is the kind of soul-level relationship Jesus calls us to, one of risk and sacrifice. If Christians read and apply what Sauls is saying, they will become life-giving agents of grace in their communities.

DANIEL DARLING
VP of Communications for the Southern Baptist Ethics & Religious Liberty Commission, author of *The Original Jesus*

In a culture that's become more fragmented and lonely, Scott provides what many of us are longing for . . . a roadmap to deep, life-giving relationships. The journey to *Befriend* will surprise us and challenge many of our assumptions, but it's exactly what we all need.

DAVID SPICKARD
President and CEO of Jobs for Life

Nothing encapsulates the understanding of Jesus and the intentional living of those who follow him more than the words *love* and *belonging*. In *Befriend* Scott Sauls gives us the courage to embrace the "us" into belonging, a belonging that echoes in the depths of true friendship. *Befriend* is an anatomy of friendship; one that leads to love, one that leads to life.

GREG FROMHOLZ
Documentary and video director, founder of Rubicon Ireland, and author of *Broken: Restoring Trust between the Sacred and the Secular*

befriend

create belonging in
an age of judgment,
isolation, and fear

Scott Sauls

Tyndale House Publishers, Inc.
Carol Stream, Illinois

Visit Tyndale online at www.tyndale.com.

TYNDALE and Tyndale's quill logo are registered trademarks of Tyndale House Publishers, Inc.

Befriend: Create Belonging in an Age of Judgment, Isolation, and Fear

Designed by Mark Anthony Lane II

Edited by Jane Vogel

Portions of chapter 1 are adapted from "On Shame and Stewardship," *The Mother and Child Project* (Zondervan: Grand Rapids, Michigan, 2015), 217–221.

A version of chapter 14 is adapted from "Meet My African American Mentor," *Heal Us, Emmanuel* (Oklahoma City, Oklahoma: White Blackbird Books, 2016), 269–278.

Library of Congress Cataloging-in-Publication Data

Names: Sauls, Scott, author.
Title: Befriend : create belonging in an age of judgment, isolation, and fear / Scott Sauls.
Description: Carol Stream, IL : Tyndale House Publishers, Inc., 2016. | Includes
   bibliographical references.
Identifiers: LCCN 2016031825 | ISBN 9781496400949 (sc)
Subjects: LCSH: Friendship—Religious aspects—Christianity.
Classification: LCC BV4647.F7 S28 2016 | DDC 241/.6762—dc23 LC record available
   at https://lccn.loc.gov/2016031825

Printed in the United States of America

22   21   20   19   18   17   16
7   6   5   4   3   2   1

CONTENTS

FOREWORD
BY ANN VOSKAMP

WHEN WE MOVED UP HERE to this neck of the woods and settled in
on our farm, there was an old farmer who lived to the west of us and
his older brother who lived to the east, and this is what we were told:

The old farmer worried that his older brother felt the ache of
aloneness when he woke up in his empty house down by Johnson's
Corner, so the farmer made sure one of his kids always dropped off
a bucket of milk every night and left it there by his brother's front
door. Said his herd of cows produced enough milk, so he wanted his
brother to swallow down and taste it, that this was a place flowing
with the milk and honey of kindness and that none of us are ever
alone.

Turned out, though, that the older brother was mighty concerned
that the farmer didn't have enough to offer around the table for his
posse of kids, so the older brother made it a habit to head up after
nightfall and leave a couple dozen eggs at the old farmer's door—
washed eggs of shades of white and paling green and earthy brown.
Said his flock of hens produced enough eggs, so he wanted his brother
to know that all needs are tucked underneath an attentive wing of
provision and that none of us are ever alone.

Then one night in early spring, so the story goes, right after
the song of the frogs had returned to the marsh at the back of Mr.
Knapp's farm and the whole dark world was being serenaded by a rising, croaking glory, it happened that the old farmer himself headed
east with a bucket of milk and the older brother was heading west
with a crate of eggs, and somewhere south of the bridge that crosses
the Maitland River, the two brothers ran right into each other. Came

face-to-face with each other in the shadows. Recognized the other simply by how similar the other's face looked to his own.

In the bluing light, the two sat down on the warm earth and listened to the symphony of frog songs and the slow opening of each other's lives. "It is best to be with those in time that we hope to be with in eternity" (Thomas Fuller).

It is best to befriend those now who we hope to be his friend for all eternity.

It is best to consider anyone a friend who drives us closer to God.

The story goes that when the sun crept up over the horizon, it found the two brothers face-to-face there where McNaught Line meets Creamery Road, found them sitting at the crossroads.

The truest Story never stops telling us:

Wherever our roads cross with others' roads, we can experience the power of the Cross.

Wherever our roads cross with others' roads, the Cross can be lifted high and lift us both up and into him.

Wherever our roads cross, the Cross can make even us friends.

I don't know if there is anyone better qualified to write this book than Scott Sauls, because I don't know a man who better incarnates the crucified Christ to everyone he meets. Scott is the very rare man who befriends everyone he meets because he walks with Christ as his friend, carries Christ's cross as his friend, extends Christ's grace and truth as the relief of friendship. Because Scott Sauls lives as a man who knows that when his path crosses anyone's, the presence of the Cross can change everything.

When my husband and I have questions that are wrestling us down, Scott is the friend we turn to. When we need a prayer warrior in the middle of the night, Scott is the friend we turn to. When we need a fellow pilgrim's hand, a redeemed saint's mind, and a pastor's heart, Scott is the friend we turn to. In the midst of a family crisis, during seasons of desperately seeking clarity, and on uphill roads through long hard nights, Scott has faithfully, time and time again, befriended our family with deeply insightful wisdom, glasses-of-cold-water refreshment and encouragement, and an extraordinarily humble and vulnerable heart that beats like Jesus, the one who calls even us friend.

Scott can write this book, one direly needed in these times, because he is a man, a father, a thought-leader, a pastor, a cultural voice, a friend direly needed for these times.

The tone of our world wounds us in a thousand ways.

The discourse of our world attempts to continuously throw us off course.

Our exchanges with one another desperately need to change—because we all are exhausted with the ache of aloneness.

And the electrifying book Scott is offering us at this crossroads has the uncommon power to completely change the dial and frequency of our personal exchanges with culture and our world—by changing the frequency of how we communicate like Christ.

In an age of isolation, judgement, and fear, these enlightening, fresh words offer the profound hope of ushering in more of a Kingdom age—an age of belonging by grace, through self-giving love, in the power of Christ.

That old farmer and his older brother—they could have missed each other in the middle of their dark nights. They could have missed meeting each other's aloneness, they could have missed meeting and caring for each other's unspoken brokenness, they could have missed letting their meeting be a holy place of rising up in the power of the Cross.

Do not miss the truly life-changing power of the words in your hands, words that echo the Word. Whoever's path you cross is meant to be transformed by the power of Cross.

So turn these rare pages with C. S. Lewis right there at your ear: "Friendship is not a reward for our discrimination and good taste in finding one another out. It is the instrument by which God reveals to each the beauties of all the others."

Who knows who you may meet along your own shadowed roads, whose face may remind you of yours and his, who you may turn to in your aloneness and smile at the unexpected relief of "friend."

Chapter One

A CASE FOR BEFRIENDING

REAL FRIENDSHIP IS HARD.

There are other, less real versions of friendship. The less real versions are "less" because they are less costly, less committed, less disruptive, less scary, less gritty, less gutsy, and less out-of-our-control than *real* friendship. But here's the rub:

Less real versions of friendship are also *less rich*. In the short run, they feel better and smoother than real friendship. But in the long run, they leave us lonely and alone. And it is not good to be alone.[1]

Less real versions of friendship take several forms.

Digital Friendship

In today's world of social media, relating to others through screens has become a chief way—and for some of us, *the* chief way—to seek connection. For example, it is not uncommon for a group of teenagers to be in the same room together as they "chat" through text messaging and social media without having a single face-to-face conversation with each other. On social media, we "friend," "like," and "follow" each other, sometimes without ever actually meeting each other. As a weekly blogger, I have what is called an online "community," but it falls short of being a *true* community because self-disclosure flows in only one direction: from my keyboard to other people's screens.

There are many positive aspects to digital friendship. But by itself, digital friendship fails as a substitute for true friendship. Unlike true friendship, relating to others through screens makes it easy for us to hide. It allows us to put forth only the best, most attractive, most "together," edited, and screened version of ourselves. When digital friendships become the main way we relate to others, a subtle but significant shift happens. Instead of entering the messiness of having real friends, we settle for having (and being) followers and fans. The chief drawback is that we never really get to know people, and they never really get to know us. Our digital friends are experiencing part of us but not all of us. When online relationships take priority over real friendship, the result is usually more loneliness and isolation, not less.

Transactional Friendship

My friend and mentor of ten years, Tim Keller, describes another less-than-real form of friendship: transactional friendship. Real friends see each other as long-term companions and give to each other the rare gift of long-term loyalty. Instead of using each other, they serve each other. Instead of keeping score with each other, they support, champion, encourage, serve, forgive, and strengthen each other. In real friendship, the flourishing of other people takes priority over our own goals and ambitions.

In contrast, transactional friendship isn't really friendship. Unlike real friendship, transactional friendship treats other people as a means to an end. When we relate this way, we come to view people more as resources than as human beings. Instead of loving and serving them as we would in a real friendship, we *use* them to advance our careers, build our platforms, gain access to their social circles, increase our self-esteem (I feel important now, because I am connected to *her*), impress others (Selfie time! Hey, everybody, look at how important I am, now that I am connected to *him*), and so on. The pitfall of transactional friendships should be obvious. As soon as a relationship feels more costly than beneficial to us, as soon as the presence of the other person in our lives ceases to advance our personal goals, we discard the other person. Or, if the opposite is true, the other person discards us.

One-Dimensional Friendship

Friendships are one-dimensional when they revolve around a single shared interest and not much else. The shared interest can be anything: a hobby, a career path, a common enemy, an educational philosophy, a set of religious beliefs, and so on. One-dimensional friendships prioritize *sameness*, so views and convictions and practices are never challenged and blind spots are never uncovered. Friendships like these can't offer the natural, redemptive, character-forming tension that diversity brings to our lives. When celebrities limit their friendships to other celebrities, parents to other parents, married people to other married people (single people, too), athletes to other athletes, Republicans to other Republicans (Democrats, too), Millennials to other Millennials (Gen Xers and Baby Boomers, too), Christians to other Christians, white people to other white people (people of color, too), thinkers to other thinkers (feelers, too), affluent people to other affluent people, and so on, a poverty of friendship will be the outcome. One-dimensional friendships, while having the appearance of connection, can also be quite shallow—unless the single dimension that initially attracts us to each other develops into other broader and deeper dimensions.

A Case for Befriending

In his magnificent book on human connection, *The Four Loves*, C. S. Lewis says that all true friendship *begins* when one person looks at another and says, "You, too?"

Starting a friendship around a common interest or passion is natural, and it is not in itself a bad thing. Consider David and Jonathan, for example. One was the son of a humble shepherd, the other the son of a king, and they became the best of friends. Though their social and economic situation was very different, their friendship nonetheless began with a "You, too?" And theirs was the most solid "You, too?" that any two people can have. Because David and Jonathan both loved and were sold out to the Lord, they became the best of friends.

Although their friendship *began* with a foundation of "You, too?" the connection between David and Jonathan grew in depth, breadth, and layers. A shared love for God matured into a reciprocal transparency, vulnerability, love, and loyalty between them that would later move David to adopt Jonathan's son, Mephibosheth, after Jonathan died in battle. Mephibosheth was a young man, crippled in both feet. But his special needs, rather than being a deterrent for David, became a motivation to mercifully take him in for the Lord's sake, and also "for Jonathan's sake."[2]

This kind of friendship—the multilayered kind that exposes us to the grit of our own and each other's lives; the kind that positions us to love across the lines of our differences; the kind that leads us to lay down our lives for each other's sake—works a lot like two pieces of sandpaper being rubbed together. The friction causes sensations that initially irritate and burn. Yet, over time, the effect on both pieces of sandpaper is the same. Both become smoother, not in spite of the friction but precisely *because* of it.

Real friends not only agree but disagree; real friends not only applaud each other's strengths but challenge each other's weaknesses; real friends not only enjoy life together but struggle through life together; real friends not only praise one another but apologize to and forgive one another; real friends not only rally around their points of agreement but love and learn from their points of disagreement. When this happens—when friendship grows beyond one dimension to many dimensions—a poverty of friendship is replaced by a richness of friendship. Digital, transactional, and one-dimensional friendship is replaced by real friendship. Everybody matures and grows. And when everybody matures and grows, everybody wins.

C. S. Lewis captured the heart of this version of friendship— real friendship—when he said the following:

> To love at all is to be vulnerable. Love anything, and your heart will certainly be wrung and possibly be broken. If you want to make sure of keeping it intact, you must give your heart to no one, not even to an animal. Wrap it carefully round with hobbies and little luxuries; avoid all entanglements; lock it up safe in the casket or coffin of your selfishness. But in that casket—safe, dark, motionless, airless—it will change. It will not be broken; it will become unbreakable, impenetrable, irredeemable.[3]

There you have it. Real love, real friendship, is vulnerable. And risky. And costly. And discomforting. And disquieting. And agitating like sandpaper sometimes.

But the alternative is a heart that ends up in a relational casket or coffin. And who wants that?

Befriend is a collection of twenty essays. Each essay attempts to explore a unique picture of *real* friendship. All of the stories are true, but some of the names and places have been changed to protect privacy.

You will notice a common thread in each account of real friendship: real friendship happens when we move *toward* the people we are most tempted to avoid. These are the people who are best equipped to challenge our perspectives, push our buttons, and require us to put on love.

Love, the Bible tells us, is the supreme virtue among all virtues. It is patient and kind. It does not envy or boast. It is not arrogant or rude. It does not demand its own way. It is not irritable or resentful. It does not rejoice at wrongdoing but rejoices with the truth. It bears all things, believes all things, hopes all things, and endures all things. It never fails.[4]

Do you know what else never fails? Or, better said, *who* else? *Jesus.* Jesus never fails.

As we take this journey of real friendship together—as we learn a little bit more about what it could look like to be those who befriend and who create belonging in a world of judgment, isolation, and fear—the icing on the cake is that we will encounter Jesus in the process.

Let's encounter Jesus together, shall we?

How to Read This Book:
The Best Option: In Community

The best way to read this book is in community with others. If possible, invite one or more people on this journey with you. Even better, invite people whose perspectives, whose ways of seeing the world and God, are in some ways different than your own: people of a different generation, a different gender, a different political persuasion, a different Myers-Briggs or enneagram profile, a different ethnicity or culture, a different career path, a different religious tradition, a different income bracket, a different level on the org chart. Then, over time and as you invest in this conversation together, watch how Jesus works in you because of them, and in them because of you. I can almost guarantee that both you and they will be changed.

The Second-Best Option: As a Daily Study

The second-best option is to read a chapter a day as a personal study. Each of the twenty-one chapters is intentionally short enough to be read easily in a day. Research suggests that it takes twenty-one days to develop a habit, so as a bonus, by the end of this book, you will have gone a long way toward developing a habit of looking at others with an embracing mind-set.

The Third-Best Option: Just Read

The third-best option would be to read *Befriend* as you would any other book . . . alone in your favorite reading spot. It's much better to read a book alone than to not read it at all!

Whatever way you choose to engage these pages, I pray that God will bless you in this journey. Please feel free to respond to anything in this book with your thoughts, encouragements, and disagreements. I can be found at Christ Presbyterian Church—my beloved community of friends—in the great city of Nashville, Tennessee (http://christpres.org).

Your friend,
Scott Sauls

— o —

SUMMARY: There is real, loyal, across-the-lines-of-differences friendship, and there is lesser, surface-level friendship. Lesser friendship leaves us distanced, isolated, and afraid. We become the best version of ourselves, and we come to know Jesus best, through real friendship.

SCRIPTURE: 2 Samuel 1:26; John 15:12-17

Greater love has no one than this, that someone lay down his life for his friends. You are my friends (John 15:13-14).

TO CONSIDER: Right now, how would you describe most of your friendships? Would you say that most of your friendships are one-dimensional or real? What scares you, and what excites you, about plunging into the rest of this book?

Chapter Two

BEFRIEND THE ONE IN THE MIRROR

ONCE A FRIEND NAMED JANE sent me the following e-mail:

Dear Scott,

Can I be honest with you? Can I share with you about some of the demons that haunt me? It feels risky to say these sorts of things to my pastor, but here goes . . .

I doubt my love for Jesus. Sometimes I don't think I really love him at all. I wonder if I'm just playing a game, going through the motions because I enjoy being around Christians. Maybe this is just a strategy to have Christian friends. Sometimes I feel like a well-intentioned fraud. This terrifies me. I fear that I'm an outsider to things I really want to be part of.

Struggling on,
Jane

This e-mail came on the heels of my challenging Jane in an area of her life. Specifically, Jane had a loose tongue. She cursed a lot and could be opinionated and abrasive. I reminded her of Scriptures about how, as the aroma of Jesus in the world, we are called to cultivate the fruit of gentleness. We are also called to mirror Jesus in our speech—with words that are grace filled, that give life instead of stealing life, that speak the truth in love, that build up and don't tear down, that encourage and don't shame, that bless and don't curse, that give a good report and don't gossip, that are pure and don't succumb to vulgarity. As Ann Voskamp has said, Jesus wants us to use our speech to make souls stronger.

After I challenged Jane on these things, I wasn't sure how she would respond. So when her e-mail landed in my in-box, I was floored. The self-reflection, transparency, heavyheartedness, and humility with which she spoke seemed like a new version of Jane—a version that I had not before experienced but one that I was drawn to. What's more, Jane's words confirmed something good for us all to remember: external bravado is often a cover-up for internal fear and insecurity; the appearance of an inflated self-esteem often camouflages an impoverished view of oneself. For Jane, what looked like bravado and pride was actually a mask for fear and self-doubt.

Hearing Jane share so openly about her hidden struggle made me love and respect her more, not less. In making herself vulnerable, she became an example to me of a person of great courage. I was proud of her. Above all, I began to relate to her. Ironically, her sober response to my correction became a soft, unintended yet Spirit-filled correction to me. I, too, am prone to hide my fear and insecurity with words and actions that betray my love for Jesus.

Jane had been abrasive for the same reasons that I will often overeat to deal with stress, dial up the intensity with a family member when I feel threatened or afraid (my wife, Patti, calls this "going from zero to sixty in two seconds"), or medicate my inner emptiness with retail therapy—buying things I don't need (a *tenth* pair of jeans and *another* pair of brown leather shoes—really?) instead of running straight to Jesus for the mending of my broken self.

We are all messed up and damaged and afraid, aren't we? We act it out in some of the oddest ways. The sooner we admit this to each other—that we are in many ways weak, restless, and much afraid—the easier it will be to love each other better.

The Sickness in Us All

According to the Bible, there is a sickness that all of us carry. It turns us inward and cripples our capacity to love well. The name for this sickness is *shame*. Shame is an emotional undercurrent—a low-grade anxiety—that nags and needles at the soul. It is a fever without a temperature, an ever-present condition that tells us we are less than, smaller than, and other than what we ought to be.

The older I get, the more convinced I become that every person, without exception, is dealing with shame. It has been said, "Be kind, because everyone you meet is fighting a hidden battle." I think that's true.

Shame—the disquieting, vague sense that there's something deeply wrong with us, *that we are not enough*—keeps us preoccupied with ourselves and inattentive to the needs of others. It tells us that we have to fix ourselves before we can serve others, to clean up messy selves before we can be any good to friends and neighbors and especially to the poor, lonely, oppressed, and people on the margins. "Charity starts at home," we tell ourselves. If something isn't done about *us* first, then we'll never be able to care effectively for others. If *we* don't get healthy, our ability to invest in anyone *besides* ourselves will be limited.

There is some truth to this, but we often compensate in ways that make things worse instead of better. When Adam and Eve's shame was exposed in the garden, their focus shifted to themselves. Adam searched for fig leaves to cover his nakedness, and Eve did the same. They ran and hid from God. They also lost interest in each other's well-being and turned against each other. Adam blamed Eve for the new predicament, then he blamed God. Eve blamed the serpent. History's first experience of hell—alienation from the face of God and love for one another—broke loose.

The story of Adam and Eve is also the story of us. We know that we aren't what we should be, so we hide, blame, run for cover, and look out for number one. When shame knocks on our door, in desperation we create counternarratives to silence it. We grasp for something to tell us that everything is okay— that *we* are okay. We will use anything—good looks, status, career, family, humor, friendships, religion, sex, influence, or a financial portfolio—to rewrite our stories. Desperately, we attempt to take shame out of our stories and replace it with these things we depend on to validate us. But it's only a matter of time before the validating "fig leaves" let us down.

Before relocating to Nashville in 2012, I was ministering in a part of New York City with a high concentration of men and women who worked in finance. When the Great Recession hit in 2008, financial institutions crashed and careers vaporized. Many people felt that they had not only lost money and a career; they had also lost a sense of self. When you work on Wall Street, eventually you start believing that you *are* what you do, and you *are* what you make. "What is she worth?" is a question that is taken literally. Human value is measured not in terms of intrinsic dignity, but in terms of salaries, bonuses, and portfolios.

When the salary and the bonus disappear and the portfolio is cut in half, one's sense of worth and personhood bleed out. A multibillionaire from London lost half of his net worth in

2008. Though he remained a multibillionaire and his quality of life was unchanged, he committed suicide. The shame of losing rank in the pecking order of the financial world drove him to self-loathing, then to despair, and finally to self-injury and destruction.

Jesus, Not Our Achievements, Gives Us Our Worth and Wealth

What if there were a way to break free from the pressures of riches and success? What if the smile of Jesus—not our financial net worth, reputation, career successes, achievements, body type, religious devotion, or moral goodness—became our source of validation? What if success was no longer measured in terms of achievement but in terms of humility, thankfulness, wonder, a life of love, and being faithful in the ordinary mundaneness of life? What if our secret battle with shame was neutered so we could spend less energy covering ourselves and more energy loving the people in front of us?

My greatest joy as a Christian pastor is telling people that this path exists. Jesus has lifted our shame off of us, nailing it to the cross.

In Jesus, our judgment day was moved from the future to the past.

Jesus, the perfect one who had nothing to be ashamed of, let himself be stripped naked, spit upon, taunted, rejected, and made nothing on the cross. When he surrendered to the ruthless shaming and bullying that led to our redemption and healing, he neutered our shame and stripped it of its power.

He who was wealthy became poor for our sakes, that through his poverty we might become wealthy (see 2 Corinthians 8:9). But the wealth that Jesus gives is a different kind of wealth. It's a shame-killing wealth. It's a love-empowering wealth. It's an inner resource that gives us certainty, protection, and validation in ways that the London billionaire's wealth couldn't give to him. When we are made wealthy in Jesus, we lose the need to validate ourselves with money, physical attractiveness, intelligence, social connections, fame, or any other thing that we have erroneously clung to for dear life.

And the "Jane" in all of us can come out of hiding and share the haunting secret: we are not self-assured but much afraid; we do not feel secure but vulnerable; we act big because we feel insignificant; we go from zero to sixty in two seconds because we fear invisibility and irrelevance. The saving, loving, forgiving wealth that Jesus gives invalidates, neuters, and disempowers these fears. It assures us that at our best and at our worst, in Jesus we are fully known *and* fully loved. In Jesus we are exposed but *not* rejected. In Jesus we can be naked and *never* ashamed.

We are free from ever having to make something *of* ourselves or to make a name *for* ourselves. We are free from having to rewrite our own stories, from having to fight shame with validating fig-leaf narratives. The name of Jesus is sufficient to name us. The story of Jesus is sufficient to be *our* story. His name liberates us from preoccupation with self. His grace and love supply the inner resources to turn our hearts and faces toward others, to treat all people as our equals, to love bold and strong.

The Dignity of All—Including the One in the Mirror

Last year at an awareness dinner in Nashville, Melinda Gates told a room full of pastors, leaders, culture makers, and influencers why she and her husband, Bill, decided to devote the rest of their lives to helping people in the developing world. Her reason was plain and simple, and it echoes truths first revealed in the earliest pages of Scripture:

All people are equal.

"There is no reason," Mrs. Gates told us, "why a woman in the developing world shouldn't have health care and education and running water and opportunity just like I do. Because a woman in the developing world is equal to me."

Dr. Martin Luther King Jr. expressed the same sentiment when he said that there are no gradations in the image of God, and therefore we are to respect the dignity and worth of every person.

C. S. Lewis, in *The Weight of Glory*, avers that next to the blessed sacrament itself, our neighbor is the holiest object presented to our senses.

These things are true about people in the developing world, the people Dr. King valiantly and prophetically defended, and those C. S. Lewis had in mind as he wrote. But there is more. These things are also true of the face you see in the mirror. These things are also true of you.

You may be asking yourself how you could possibly take the focus off of yourself, forget the fig leaves, and start loving boldly and broadly. It begins with the recognition that you, too, have been loved . . . to the fullest extent! You, too, bear the image of God. You, too, are the crown of his creation. You, too, are valuable, highly esteemed, of great significance and worth, a holy object, a person created to be loved.

As the late Francis Schaeffer said, there are no little people. *You are not little.* You are not invisible or insignificant or irrelevant.

So whenever you have a "Jane moment," whenever you look in the mirror and feel terribly discouraged, whenever you feel tired of yourself—don't forget that in Jesus, you are highly esteemed. Don't forget that in Jesus, with you the Father is well pleased. Don't forget that you, who are small in your own eyes, are big in the eyes of God. Big enough for him to see. Big enough for him to love. Big enough for him to save. He so loved you that he gave his Son for you. You are the apple of his eye. He rejoices over you with singing.[1]

And now, in light of these great realities, O child of God, he has also given you a job to do: to start loving as you have been loved.

— o —

SUMMARY: Sometimes the greatest barrier to loving is a vague belief that we are ourselves unlovable. It is *shame* that makes us feel this way.

SCRIPTURE: Zephaniah 3:17; John 3:16
[God] will take great delight in you . . . [he] will rejoice over you with singing (Zephaniah 3:17, NIV).

TO CONSIDER: What keeps you from loving every kind of person whom Jesus loves? Specifically, how does shame contribute to the limits you place upon your love? How can belief in the Bible's teaching on the image of God and the far-reaching love of God broaden your limits and open up your boundaries?

Chapter Three

BEFRIEND THE "OTHER"

ONCE MY WIFE, PATTI, AND I were in a small prayer gathering with some friends. Just before we began praying together, in came a husband and a wife that we had never met. They had been invited by someone else in the group. The man's name was Matthew, and he was drunk. His wife had a desperate *somebody-please-help-me-because-I'm-dying-inside* look on her face.

As we prayed together, Matthew decided to chime in. His was a drunk prayer that went on for over ten minutes. He prayed some of the strangest things. *God, protect us from the Klingons. God, I really want a Jolly Rancher right now, will you bring us some Jolly Ranchers? God, please move my bananas to the doghouse.*

After the "Amen," everyone looked at me. What will the pastor do? Thankfully, I didn't need to do anything, because a woman from the group, full of love and wisdom, offered Matthew a cookie. As the woman was giving him a cookie and entertaining conversation about Klingons and such, five or six others went over to his wife and begged for insight on how they could help the situation.

Lessons from a Drunk Man at a Prayer Meeting

Where did this woman learn such a gracious way of befriending Matthew? From Jesus.

Don't you love how Jesus welcomed the outsiders inside, how he invited them to belong before they believed?

A woman is caught in the act of adultery. She sins against God. She wrecks a home. She brings shame on herself and to her community. Pious men make her shame public. *Lawbreakers must not be tolerated. She must be condemned for her behavior, cast out for her infidelities, shamed for her shameful act. She must be made into an example.*

This is what happens in groups with a narrow "us." A coliseum culture forms. The mob organizes. A common enemy is named and the caricature is established. *The woman caught in adultery. The sinner.* Not a person, but a thing. Not a she, but an it. Not an image bearer, but an animal. Not a woman, but a whore. Then the pouncing. Then the shame.

But not Jesus. Jesus, left alone with the woman, simply says to her two things: "I do not condemn you. Now leave your life of sin." The order is everything. Reverse the order of these two sentences, and we lose Christianity and get rigid, religious moralism in its place. Reverse the order and we lose Jesus.

God demonstrates his own love for us in this: While we were still sinners, Christ died for us.
ROMANS 5:8, NIV

Whenever our heart condemns us, God is greater than our heart. 1 JOHN 3:20

Wherever love dominates the environment, it's *no condemnation* first and ethics after that. With Jesus, love establishes the environment for the morality conversation. It is not our repentance that leads to God's kindness, but God's kindness that leads to our repentance.

After eighteen years of pastoral ministry, I have never met a person who fell in love with Jesus because a Christian scolded them about their ethics. Have you?

That little interaction at the prayer meeting, that way of responding with love and *no condemnation* first, became one of the most transformative experiences I have ever witnessed. The kindhearted offer of a cookie led to a different kind of mob—a mob of grace coming around the couple and their two young boys, which led to a month of rehab, which led to sobriety, which led to a restored home and marriage, which led to Matthew becoming a follower of Jesus, which led to him later becoming an elder in the church.

Grace comes before ethics. *No condemnation* comes before the morality discussion. Kindness leads to repentance. Love— the broad embrace of Jesus' narrow path—creates the most life-giving experiences you'll ever be part of.

Eulogy Virtues

At a conference in 2014, *New York Times* writer David Brooks gave a fascinating talk called "How to Be Religious in the Public Square," in which he said that we live in an achievement culture, where success is our primary pursuit. We live by two sets of virtues: the résumé virtues—things we bring to the marketplace—and the eulogy virtues—things we want said about us at our funerals. Brooks concludes, "In [our] secular achievement culture, we all know the eulogy virtues are more important, but we spend more time on the résumé virtues."[1]

The résumé virtues—the ones that drive things like calling, creativity, and achievement—lead people to do some extraordinary things that make the world better. However, when the résumé virtues are the sole focus, or even the primary one, poor and regrettable outcomes tend to follow. Who wants a tombstone that reads, "He spent many hours at the office and away from his loved ones, accomplishing much and earning huge bonuses"? And yet, at the deathbed, many of us will look back on such a life and be haunted by regret.

In 1 Corinthians, we are told that we can have rich skill sets, decorated résumés, even exemplary commitments to morality and biblical law-keeping, but if we don't have love, we gain nothing and we are nothing. This has the potential to dawn on us at the end of our lives, when it's too late. This book is written to help us—to help me—avoid this regrettable end. This book is written to help us start living a full life, an abundant life, a truly faithful life now. We can live a love-shaped life, a life into which Love himself invites us.

Aim at the eulogy virtues, and you'll get the résumé virtues thrown in.

Throughout Scripture, we are told that love is the ultimate virtue. All the commands, the entire blueprint of what it means to be truly and fully human, Jesus said, are summed up in love for God and love for neighbor. It is God's love that compelled him to send his Son to save a broken humanity, to rescue us from ourselves. It is a life of love that determines truest success. The résumé virtues matter because God made us vocational beings and calls us into his mission to renew and restore all things. However, the eulogy virtue—agape love—reigns supreme. Without love, our skill sets and even our morals are bereft of power. But with love, we have within us a power that can heal the world.

Heavenly Father,
Grant me character that exceeds my gifts.
Grant me humility that exceeds my platform.

Lessons from a Broken Church

The prophet Jeremiah writes that the heart has great potential for self-deception. We can be accomplishing good things in life and be doing all the "right things"—attending church, serving in ministry, studying Scripture, praying daily, feeding the hungry, helping the weak, preaching solid theology, correcting bad theology, leading people to Jesus—but still be missing the mark. When writing to the Corinthians, Paul boils it down to this: *love for God is verified by love for neighbor.*

In Corinth, neighbor-love had been hijacked. Church members were judging each other, dividing over minor doctrinal issues, committing adultery, suing each other, divorcing without biblical grounds, parading their Christian liberty before those with tender consciences, ignoring the poor in their midst, and drawing lines around the Eucharist that were tighter than the lines drawn by Jesus . . . excluding from *his* table those whom *he* was passionate to include.

Instead of expanding their "us," they narrowed it.

How does Paul confront the Corinthians' inconsistency and lack of love? In 1 Corinthians 13 he paints a vivid picture of love, that stunning, ever-inspiring catalog of attributes—patience, kindness, humility, generosity of spirit, preferring others, a peaceful demeanor, love for truth, readiness to bear and believe and hope and endure all things. Paul didn't have weddings in mind when he wrote this. This is actually one of the sharpest rebukes in the Bible, because the attributes of love described everything that the Corinthians were not.

> When you come together as a church . . . there are divisions among you . . . factions. . . . When you come together, it is not the Lord's Supper that you eat.
> I CORINTHIANS II:18-20

But when love is in the air, everything changes. When love is in the air, divisions and factions fade. When love is in the air, we are moved to expand our "us." When love is in the air, the Supper becomes Love's Supper again: the agape feast that welcomes all who believe, recline, and receive; the love feast that holds a seat for God's workmanship from every nation, tribe, and tongue, for every hero with a decorated résumé and every sinner with a damaged one, for the affluent and the poor, the confident believers and the struggling doubters.

[They] muttered, "This man welcomes sinners and eats with them." LUKE 15:2, NIV

The more we walk the narrow path, the wider our communal embrace will be. The more convinced we are of the exclusive claims of Jesus—that he is the way, the truth, and the life and no one comes to the Father except through him—the more inclusively kind and compassionate we will be. The more attuned we are to Jesus' bleeding love toward us, the more our hearts will bleed for those who don't know his embrace.

Grace comes before ethics. *No condemnation* comes before the morality discussion. Kindness leads to repentance. Love—the broad embrace of Jesus' narrow path, the supreme eulogy virtue—creates the most life-giving experiences you'll ever be part of.

Love Is a Battlefield

Singers and songwriters portray love in many different ways. Tina Turner says love is a secondhand emotion. Chaka Khan says she feels for you, and on the basis of this, she thinks she loves you. But maybe Pat Benatar was the one whose vision for love was the most in line with Jesus. Because Pat Benatar said that *love is a battlefield.*

Love is hard. It's a battlefield because love—*agape*—is the word Jesus uses when he tells us to love our enemies and pray for those who persecute us. When love takes on this definition, it becomes much more than a feeling. Words like *tenacious, resilient, gutsy, vulnerable*, and *selfless* come to mind. Agape love—the eulogy love that is stronger than death, that saves sinners, that gives adulteresses hope, that makes drunk men sober, that will redeem the universe—this love is countercultural. It is otherworldly in its nature because its truest test comes when we *don't* feel warm personal attachment or deep affection toward the beloved. Eulogy-virtue love is a *cruciform* love, the kind that compels us to broaden our embrace, to move toward the "other," to include the "other" in our "us" because Jesus has included us in his. The hard love, the battlefield love, the tenacious and strong love, *agape*—this is the love that leads Jesus and the people of Jesus to love their persecutors even better than their persecutors love each other.

Earlier this year, Patti and I had the privilege of having dinner with Rich Stearns, president of World Vision. World Vision is a leader in mercy and justice efforts around the world. My fork fell out of my hand when Rich Stearns put words to his redemptive imagination in order to stimulate ours as well: "Imagine Christians feeding Syrian Muslims while ISIS beheads Christians."

Does love go this far? *Can* love go this far? *Should* love go this far?

Love *did* go this far.

Loving like Jesus—Is It Possible?

How do we become the kinds of people—the kinds of lovers—who form a grace mob that silences the shame mob, who respond to a drunk husband with cookies and commitment, who feed and bless and pray for those intent on hurting us? How does this kind of love flourish?

There is only one way. We must become convinced that Love has to be a person to us before it can become a verb. The one who *is* Love incarnate—Jesus—doesn't love us only when we're at our best. He also loves us when we are at our worst. When we are caught in the act. When we fall asleep instead of watching and praying with him. When we deny him three times. When we become his persecutors. When we come into his prayer meetings drunk—drunk on our ambition, our greed, our resentful grudges, our pornographic imaginations, our self-righteousness. From *these places* he asks, "Do you like cookies? May I get you one? Will you sit with me? How about rehab—may I accompany you there? May I pay the fee? May I come alongside you toward sobriety, then a new life, then a seat at my Table, then a job in my Kingdom? I went to the battlefield, I loved from the battlefield, to set this love trajectory for your life. Protection from the Klingons. Sweeter than Jolly Ranchers. All you need is nothing. All you need is need."

All the fitness he requires is for you to feel your need of him.

How do we love like Jesus?

It starts with resting and receiving. It starts by stopping.

Maybe before we can love *like* Jesus, we need to learn what it means to be *with* him.

Because the more we are with Jesus, the more we will become like him. Love is caught more than it is achieved. Get close to Love, and love tends to rub off.

Let's pursue this path, the love path, the eulogy path . . . shall we?

— o —

SUMMARY: True success is measured not by skill sets, achievements, or religious morality, but by love. The power for loving comes from knowing that Jesus first loved us, and entering into an experience of his love.

SCRIPTURE: Psalm 63:1-8; 1 Corinthians 13:1-13
If I have prophetic powers, and understand all mysteries and all knowledge, and if I have all faith, so as to remove mountains, but have not love, I am nothing (1 Corinthians 13:2).

TO CONSIDER: Right now, where is your greatest opportunity to expand your "us"? Is there someone who needs to hear a hopeful verdict, to be surprised by warmth and welcome, to be forgiven, to be loved? Who is it, and what would be a loving first step?

Chapter Four

BEFRIEND PRODIGALS AND PHARISEES

ARCHBISHOP WILLIAM TEMPLE once said that the Christian Church, in its purest form, is the only society that exists for the benefit of its nonmembers. Though some Christians over the centuries have fallen into an "us-only" way of living, no one can dispute that Jesus prioritized the outsider. I suppose you could say that he was always looking to expand his "us."

In his living, his teaching, and his loving, Jesus was attractive to the nonreligious and moral outcasts of his day. Tax collectors and sinners were *all* drawing near to be with him. But the Pharisees and scribes—the religious leaders, the faithful churchgoers, the ones who gave their tithes and studied their Bibles and built their identity on *being right*—were suspicious of Jesus. When outsiders drew near to him, the Pharisees and scribes grumbled, "This man receives sinners and eats with them."

Jesus became a scandal among the religious and the upright not because of actual guilt, but because of guilt by association. When sinners invited him to their parties, he went.

When people of ill repute came near, he invited them into friendship.

> The Son of Man has come eating and drinking, and
> you say, "Look at him! A glutton and a drunkard,
> a friend of tax collectors and sinners!" LUKE 7:34

Of course Jesus was neither a glutton nor a drunk. But a friend of tax collectors and sinners? Yes, indeed.

My friend and former professor Phil Douglas is known for saying that a love for lost people covers over a multitude of sins. This is Phil's way of saying that God, who *so loved* the world, gave his Son in order to seek and save the lost and to make a way for every type of person—conservative and liberal, affluent and bankrupt, happy and depressed, with PhDs and with special needs, healthy and addicted, on the move and tired, secular and religious, approachable and angry at the universe—to join the sacred communion of Father, Son, and Spirit. Not as servants in his Kingdom but as heirs to his Kingdom. Not as bastards but as his beloved daughters and sons. Not as prostitutes but as his bride, his cherished queen.

A Junkie, a Cussing Mom, and a Church Guy

Once during a church service, a well-groomed man I will call "Church Guy" tapped me on the shoulder during the singing. He pointed to a man that neither of us had ever seen before—a first-time visitor.

"Do you see that man?" Church Guy asked. "Can you believe that he would come into the house of God with those dirty jeans and that ratty T-shirt and drinking coffee like that? And when he passed me in the hallway, he reeked of nicotine. Pastor, what are you going to do about that man? He is a distraction to my worship."

All heaven started to weep.

My brothers, show no partiality . . . if a man wearing a
gold ring and fine clothing comes into your assembly,
and a poor man in shabby clothing also comes in, and
. . . you say to the poor man, "You stand over there . . . "
have you not then made distinctions among yourselves
and become judges with evil thoughts? Listen, my
beloved brothers, has not God chosen those who are poor
in the world to be rich in faith and heirs of the kingdom?

JAMES 2:1-9

A distraction to worship? This shabbily-dressed, coffee-drinking, nicotine-stained man may have actually been an ambassador of Jesus in our midst.

Truly, I say to you, as you did it to one of the least
of these my brothers, you did it to me.

MATTHEW 25:40

Thankfully, after the service, another church member got to our visitor before Church Guy could. The church member, himself a recovering alcoholic, warmly welcomed the visitor, got his name, and asked him about his story.

The visitor's name was George. He was recovering from a heroin addiction and felt like being part of a church could help him with that.

What do you call a nicotine addiction for a man who is recovering from heroin? You call it victory. You call it progress. You call it an upgrade.

That same Sunday, a woman named Janet, also a first-time visitor, dropped her two boys off in the nursery. After the service, while she was waiting in the nursery line to retrieve her boys, one of the nursery workers quietly approached her and said that there had been some issues. Both of her boys had picked fights with other children. Also, one of her boys had broken several of the toys that belonged to the church.

In front of a room filled with other children and their parents, Janet scolded her boys and then screamed in a bellowing voice, "S—!"

Deeply ashamed and feeling like a failure, Janet got her boys and skulked out of the building. No doubt, we were never going to see her again.

The nursery worker called the church office that Monday and asked if I could check the visitor notebook to see if Janet had left her contact information. She had. I gave the nursery worker Janet's address, and unbeknownst to me, she sent Janet a note. The note read something like this:

Dear Janet,

I'm so glad that you and your boys visited our church. Oh, and about that little exchange when you picked them up from the nursery? Let's just say that I found it so refreshing—that you would feel freedom to speak with an honest vocabulary like that in church. I am really drawn to honesty, and you are clearly an honest person. I hope we can become friends.

Love,
The nursery worker

The nursery worker and Janet did in fact become friends. Janet came back the next Sunday. And the Sunday after that. And the Sunday after that. And eventually, Janet became the nursery director for the church.

There's another significant detail about Janet's story. She is also George's wife. And when she first came to us, she, too, was recovering from heroin.

The Largest Donation Ever

About a year after I first met George and Janet at church, they called me and asked for a meeting at Starbucks. At the meeting, George looked at me across the table nervously and said, "Pastor, our church means so much to us. The love we have received from this community has been such an important part of our recovery, and we wanted to do something to say thank you. I come from a very wealthy family, and Janet and I just received a large inheritance. We would like to give some of that to the church."

George handed me a check. It was made out to the church in the amount of fifty dollars. As far as I am concerned, that fifty dollars is the most significant gift ever given to any church, anywhere.

A full tithe? I doubt it. Technically correct according to biblical guidelines for giving? Not even close. But the trajectory of George's and Janet's hearts in that moment was monumental. It was a sign of the Kingdom that starts small but that grows into something mighty over time.

I can't help but wonder if in that moment, George and Janet were closer to the Kingdom of God than the Church Guy—who had attended church and given a full tithe all of his life—had ever been.

> Jesus said to the Pharisees, "I assure you: tax collectors and prostitutes are entering the kingdom of God before you!"
>
> MATTHEW 21:31, HCSB

Jesus and the Church Guy

What does Jesus think of the Church Guy? What should *we* think of the Church Guy? I must admit that I left that Sunday feeling very cynical, wishing that the Church Guy wasn't part of the church—wasn't part of "us."

And yet, as I continued down the path of cynicism about the Church Guy—that the problem with the world is people *like that man*—I realized that I, too, was *becoming* the Church Guy.

As Anne Lamott says, "You can safely assume you've created God in your own image when it turns out that God hates all the same people you do."[1]

Did you know that there is such a thing as a grace-Pharisee? A grace-Pharisee is anyone who becomes an unloving Pharisee toward unloving Pharisees.

> When [Jesus] saw the crowds [many of them Pharisees and scribes], he had compassion for them, because they were harassed and helpless, like sheep without a shepherd.
>
> MATTHEW 9:36

When Jesus saw a city filled with people like the Church Guy, *he wept over that city* (Luke 19:41).

So Jesus told his story about a father and his two lost sons—one a prodigal and the other a Pharisee. The Pharisee-son refuses to attend the homecoming party for the prodigal. The dirty jeans and T-shirt and the smell of nicotine and booze and prostitutes and addiction wafting off him are just too much to take. *All this fanfare for HIM, and I—the good and pious and dutiful son, the son who kept all the rules while the other son was out breaking the rules, the son who has never once left home—I have never been given so much as a goat.* So the father leaves the ninety-nine inside the party to go after the one on the outside. He entreats his grumpy, judgmental, entitled boy in a gentle tone, "My son, you are always with me, and all that is mine is yours. It was fitting to celebrate and be glad, for this your brother was dead, and is alive; he was lost, and is found" (Luke 15:31-32).

Be kind. Everyone you meet is fighting a hidden battle.

Hurting people hurt people.

Judgmental Church Guys are fighting a hidden battle. Judgmental Church Guys are hurting too.

The Pharisee in us—the smug law-Pharisee *and* the dismissive grace-Pharisee—mistakenly believes it is his job to decide who is in and who is out. The Pharisee separates the world into *us* and *them*, the *good* people and the *bad* people. But Jesus. Jesus! *Jesus* separates the world into the proud and the humble. He joyfully and longingly expands his "us" to welcome the junkies and the cussing moms . . . and also the judgmental Church Guys.

Are we prepared to do the same?

— o —

SUMMARY: The narrow path of Jesus demands the widest embrace. The more attuned our hearts are to his, the more hope we will have for and the more love we will extend to the prodigals and Pharisees in our midst.

SCRIPTURE: Psalm 40:17; Luke 15:1-7, 25-32
As for me, I am poor and needy, but the Lord takes thought for me (Psalm 40:17).

TO CONSIDER: With whom do you identify the most—the law-Pharisee or the grace-Pharisee? What would motivate you to show love to people you are tempted to judge the most? What will be your first step?

Chapter Five

BEFRIEND THE WRECKED
AND THE RESTLESS

ONE DAY IN MY MIDTWENTIES while studying to become a pastor, I came across a suicide note published in the local newspaper—a note written by a pastor:

> *God forgive me for not being any stronger than I am. But*
> *when a minister becomes clinically depressed, there are*
> *very few places where he can turn to for help. . . . It feels as*
> *if I'm sinking farther and farther into a downward spiral*
> *of depression. I feel like a drowning man, trying frantically*
> *to lift up my head to take just one more breath. But one*
> *way or another, I know I am going down.*

The writer was the promising young pastor of a large, thriving church in St. Louis. After secretly battling depression for a long time—having sought help through prayer, therapy, and medication—he no longer had the will to claw through yet another day. In his darkest hour, the young man decided he would rather join the angels than continue facing demons for years to come. The sign-off to his note, "Yours in the Name of Our Blessed Lord, Our Only Hope in Life and Death," brought me a strange comfort, because grace covers all types of things, including suicide. Yet grief and confusion remained.

My confusion escalated when another pastor, also from St. Louis, asphyxiated himself to death because of a similar, secret depression.

The news of these two pastor suicides rocked my world. How could these men—both gifted pastors who believed in Jesus, preached grace, and comforted others with gospel hope— end up *losing* hope for themselves?

I had also heard teaching—which I have come now to believe is unbiblical and destructive—that being a Christian and being depressed and suicidal aren't supposed to go together. "Light always drives out darkness," these teachers would say. "When you're believing the right things, peace and joy will necessarily follow." Based on these ideas, a worship song was released that became very popular among Christians. The lyrics included the confident declaration that "in his presence, our problems disappear."

But when the real world hits, those teachings and songs hurt more than they help. Two faithful pastors who prayed and read their Bibles every day, who served their churches and cities and counseled people and preached grace, ended their lives . . . because in his presence, their problems did *not* disappear.

Anxiety and Depression: Two Strange Friends

I, too, have faced the demons of anxiety and depression. Most of the time, thankfully, my struggle has been more low-grade than intense. On one occasion, though, it flattened me physically, emotionally, and spiritually.

How bad was it? I could not fall asleep for two weeks straight. Even sleeping pills couldn't calm the adrenaline and knock me out. At night I was fearful of the quiet, knowing I was in for another all-night battle with insomnia that I was likely to lose. The sunrise also frightened me, an unwelcome reminder that another day of impossible struggle was ahead of me. I lost fifteen percent of my body weight in just two months. I could not concentrate in conversations. I found no comfort in God's promises from Scripture. I couldn't bring myself to pray anything but *Help* and *End this*.

According to a study conducted by researcher Thom Rainer, circumstance-triggered anxiety and depression hit ministers at a higher rate than the general populace. Due to the unique pressures associated with spiritual warfare, unrealistic expectations from congregants and oneself, growing platforms for unaccountable criticism and gossip toward and about ministers (especially in the digital age), failure to take time off for rest and replenishment, marriage difficulties, financial strains, and the problem of comparison with other ministers and ministries, ministers are set up as prime candidates for descent into an emotional abyss, Rainer suggests.[1]

The two pastors who committed suicide did so because they could not imagine navigating the emotional abyss for another day. Both also suffered their affliction in silence, for fear of being rejected. The one who left the suicide note said that if a pastor tells anyone about his depression, he's likely to lose his ministry. People don't want to be pastored, taught, or led by a damaged person.

Or do they?

Maybe instead of labeling anxious and depressed people as "damaged goods," we should learn from the Psalms and Jesus and Paul about the biblical theology of weakness. Maybe we should start learning how to apply that theology to our lives and also to the lives of those who are called to lead us. The apostle Paul said that it is in weakness that we experience the glory, power, and grace of God. This is how God works. God is upside down to our sensibilities. Better said, we are upside down to his.

Solidarity with Giants

Anne Lamott has been quoted as saying that it's okay to realize that you are crazy and very damaged, because all the best people are. Suffering has a way of equipping us to be the best expressions of God's compassion and grace. It has a way of equipping us to love and lead in ways that are helpful and not harmful. A healer who has not been wounded is extremely limited in her or his ability to heal.

In Scripture, the "crazy and very damaged" people are the ones through whom God did the greatest things. Hannah had bitterness of soul over infertility and a broken domestic situation. Elijah felt so beaten down that he asked God to take his life. Job and Jeremiah cursed the day that they were born. David repeatedly asked his own soul why it was so downcast. Even Jesus, the perfectly divine human, lamented that his soul was overwhelmed with sorrow. He wept when his friend died. Each of these biblical saints was uniquely empowered by God to change the world—not in spite of affliction, but because of it and through it.

Charles Spurgeon, the prince of preachers, was depressed during many of his best ministry years. William Cowper, the great hymn writer, had crippling anxiety for most of his adult life. Artist Vincent van Gogh checked in to an insane asylum and created some of his best paintings there. C. S. Lewis lost his wife to cancer and fell apart emotionally. Joni Eareckson Tada became paralyzed as a teenager and, for a time, became deeply depressed. My dear friend Ann Voskamp has written candidly and often about her own emotional battles and scars. *These* are the instruments God has chosen to bring truth, beauty, grace, and hope into the world. The best therapists and counselors have themselves been in therapy and counseling. It's how God works.

If you experience anxiety and depression, I am sharing this part of my story to remind you that there is no shame in having this or any other affliction. In fact, our afflictions may be the key to our fruitfulness as carriers of Jesus' love. What feels like the scent of death to us may end up becoming the scent of life for others as we learn to comfort others in their affliction with the comfort that we, in our affliction, have received from God. I'll never forget when Rick Warren eulogized his son Matthew, who from a desperate place took his own life. Rick said that Matthew was proof positive that even broken trees bear fruit. It was not in spite of his affliction, but through his affliction, that Matthew's life brought gospel hope to many strugglers.

In my darkest hour, in those months of facing into the abyss, there were two people who put themselves on permanent call for me. These two carried me day and night, with constant reminders that though I was down, I was not out. Though I was afraid, I was not alone. Though I had to face some demons, I was surrounded by an angelic presence. Perhaps these two, also, were my guardian angels.

These two were my brother, Matt, and my wife, Patti. Both were outstanding healers because both had suffered with anxiety and depression too.

Afflicted does not mean *ineffective*.

Damaged does not mean *done*.

Anxiety and depression can also, ironically, be an occasion for hope. After I had been serving about two years as pastor at Christ Presbyterian Church in Nashville, one of our members told me that he thinks I am a really good preacher . . . *and that he is entirely unimpressed by this*. He told me that the moment he decided to trust me, the moment he decided that I was *his* pastor, was when I told the whole church that I have struggled with anxiety and depression and that I have seen therapists for many years.

That's when it dawned on me. My afflictions may end up having greater impact than my preaching or my vision ever will. It is helpful to remember that most of the psalms were written from dark, depressed, wrecked, and restless places.

An Invitation to Rest

Anxiety and depression are also invitations to Sabbath rest. When you are laid flat and there's nothing you can do except beg for help, Jesus meets you in that place. It is from there that he summons the weary and heavy laden and the wrecked and restless to come to him and learn from him, to see and savor his humility and gentleness of heart . . . that we might find rest for our souls (see Matthew 11:28-30).

For an anxious, depressed person, there is nothing quite like an easy yoke and a light burden under which to process the pain.

Often anxiety and depression have come upon me when I have lost my way. Instead of resting in Jesus, I have sought validation from the crowds, wanting fans instead of friends, wanting to make a name for myself instead of making the name of Jesus famous. This is always a dead-end street, but there are times when my heart still goes there.

Anxiety and depression have been God's way of reminding me that I don't have to be awesome. He has not called me to be influential or spoken well of and liked or a celebrity who is famous like a rock star. He has foremost called me to be loved, to be receptive *to* his love, and to find my rest *in* his love. He has called me to remember that because of Jesus, I already have a name. I will be remembered and celebrated and sung over even after I am long gone, because he is my God and I am his person. He is my Father and I am his son, and on that day into eternity, there will be no more death, mourning, crying, or pain.

As the little girl once recited for her Sunday school teacher, "The Lord is my Shepherd; that's all I want." Sometimes the misquotes are the best and truest quotes, yes?

Søren Kierkegaard said that the thorn in his foot enabled him to spring higher than anyone with sound feet. The apostle Paul said something similar about the thorn in his flesh. That thorn kept him from becoming prideful. It kept him humble. It kept him fit for God and fit for the people whom God had called him to love and serve. There is glory in weakness. There is a power that is made perfect in that place (see 2 Corinthians 12:7-10).

Though I would not wish anxiety or depression on anyone, I am strangely thankful for the unique way that this affliction has led me, time and again, back into the rest of God.

As my friend and mentor Tim Keller is fond of saying:

All you need is nothing. All you need is need.

— o —

SUMMARY: God's power is made perfect in weakness. Seasons of suffering prepare us to comfort others in their struggles.

SCRIPTURE: Psalm 13; 2 Corinthians 12:7-10
For the sake of Christ, then, I am content with weaknesses, insults, hardships, persecutions, and calamities. For when I am weak, then I am strong (2 Corinthians 12:10).

TO CONSIDER: Have you been through a season of feeling "wrecked and restless"? Are there signs of God's presence and care in that season that you can thank him for now? Or, if there is still confusion and bewilderment, which particular truths and which particular friends would be helpful to surround yourself with?

Chapter Six

BEFRIEND THE SHAMED AND ASHAMED

I'LL NEVER FORGET when Mariah Carey, then a beloved diva who had more number-one hits than anyone in the history of music except for Elvis Presley and the Beatles, said in an interview that she can hear a thousand praises and just one criticism, and the criticism will completely drown out the voices of the thousand praises.[1]

Ever since that interview, I have had a special fondness for Mariah Carey. Not only did she tell the honest truth about herself . . . she also told the honest truth about me.

Most of the time, I walk around with a lurking and unsettling feeling of shame. Usually the feeling is vague, but it's there as a constant undercurrent. When I get an e-mail and the subject line says, "We need to talk" or "About your sermon," my impulse is to start panicking. Before I even know what the person wants to discuss, my internal voice starts shouting, "Sauls, you have blown it this time." The same thing happens when I discover that a new review has been written for one of my books or a new comment has come in for one of my blog posts. It's as if I'm hardwired to expect accusation and condemnation. Most of the time it ends up being the opposite. But I still expect it. There's a part of me that's constantly waiting for the shoe to drop, to be exposed and rejected, known and not loved.

In the online world especially, there are forms of passive-aggressive shaming that leave people feeling wounded and isolated. One person experiences shame when her e-mails, social media messages, and texts are ignored. Another experiences shame when he notices an unflattering photograph of him, posted without his permission and clearly shared from a motive to mock and embarrass. Another is intentionally excluded from a group selfie to convey the message, "You are *not* one of us."

Active-aggressive shaming is more direct. The angry blog, the critical tweet, the vicious comment on social media, or whatever the method—people try to hurt people. Sometimes the shaming gains momentum and develops into a mob, a faux-community that latches on to the negative verdict and piles on. Under the pretense of righteous indignation, the mob licks its chops as it goes about demonizing, diminishing, and destroying its chosen target.

The Destructive Power of Shame

Shame, whether it comes from the outside or from within, has great power over us emotionally. We are hardwired to hear the voice of shame as the loudest of all voices. It's as if the volume is turned all the way down for praise and affirmation and all the way up for condemnation.

Pastor Andy Stanley once said in a sermon that it would take just five poorly chosen words, spoken in the wrong setting, to destroy him personally and professionally.

This nightmare became true for Justine Sacco, a PR consultant who posted a single, poorly worded and easy-to-

misinterpret tweet—just twelve words to her 170 followers—
while boarding a flight to South Africa. When her plane
landed, she discovered that her words had gone viral. In a
few short hours she had become the headline, the inhumane
bigot and common enemy to tens of thousands of people.
On the basis of those twelve words, Ms. Sacco lost her career
and the life she once knew. Anything good she had done prior
to the infamous tweet became as a vapor. Looking back on
the incident, she reflected:

> I had a great career, and I loved my job, and it was
> taken away from me, and there was a lot of glory in
> that. Everybody else was very happy about that.[2]

Imagine for a moment. Your entire life, all you have ever
done or worked for, suddenly reduced to a single, ten-second,
careless mistake. And those who brought you down? They never
met or heard of you *before* today, and will never again think of
you *after* today. To those who brought you down, your name
was never sacred. Your character assassins will never have to look
you in the eye. Nor will they be held accountable for turning
your life upside down or for their blatant disregard for your
whole, image-of-God-bearing person.

New York Times writer Tim Kreider coined the term *outrage
porn* to describe what he sees as our insatiable search for things
to be offended by. Based on hundreds of comments and letters
to the editor, Kreider says that many contemporary people feed
off of being wronged and proven right.[3] Outrage porn resembles
actual pornography. It aims for a cheap thrill at the expense of
another human being but without any personal accountability
or commitment *to* that human being.

Outrage porn is not new. Similar to those who shame and
publicly air their grievances today, the New Testament Pharisees

were also known to look down on others with contempt. It's there in Simon the Pharisee as he shames the woman anointing Jesus with perfume and washing his feet with her tears and hair. She is "a sinner." Not a person, but a thing. Not a woman, but an animal. Not the image of God, but subhuman trash. It's also there in those who brand the woman caught in adultery with a scarlet letter. The mob encircles her, ready to pile on and destroy.[4] Had Jesus not intervened, one imagines that they would have destroyed her just like the Internet mob destroyed Justine Sacco for her single act, *the act that she apologized for through tears.*

But apologies don't make good stories, do they? They aren't as tweetable.

What Our Shame and Shaming Tell Us about Ourselves

The pious Pharisee's bravado and righteous indignation is merely a mask for self-justification. Forming a mob around a common enemy—around "the sinners"—was the groupthink of insecure, small-minded men. They were looking for a way to medicate their fragile egos at the expense of a scapegoat—a scapegoat who was no more shame-worthy than they.

When we are tempted to join the mob and to shame, it's important for us to shift our eyes away from our computer screens and handheld devices and to turn our eyes toward the mirror instead. It's important to get to the bottom of why we, too, enjoy the caricature and the labeling, and why we, too, are prone to "Like" and "Share" when someone else's whole life is reduced to their most foolish, offensive—and profusely-apologized-for-through-tears-like-Justine-Sacco-did —public moment.

Therapist, speaker, and author Brené Brown answers the "Why do we shame others?" question as follows:

After studying vulnerability, shame, and authenticity for the past decade, here's what I've learned. A deep sense of love and belonging is an irreducible need of all people. We are biologically, cognitively, physically, and spiritually wired to love, to be loved, and to belong. When those needs are not met, we don't function as we were meant to. We break. We fall apart. We numb. We ache. *We hurt others.*[5]

There you have it. We shame and respond unlovingly to others because deep down, we feel that our own need for love and belonging are not being met. We shame because *we* feel ashamed. We hurt because *we* are hurting. When we accuse and tear others down with words, when we gossip and slander instead of sharing our concerns directly and privately and in love, when we nurse, enforce, and broadcast our grudges instead of forgiving as God in Christ has forgiven us,[6] it shows that we, too, are dealing with the demons of shame.

Shame is the reason we feel bad when others are winning and happy when others are losing. Once I was watching the news when it was reported that Tom Hanks had fallen off of the Top 500 Celebrities list. And do you want to know how messed up I am? When I read that news about Tom Hanks, I felt good inside. A sick kind of good, that is.

Feeling that brief jolt of satisfaction over what must have felt like shame to a famous celebrity exposed something deeply broken about me. There is this part of me that is comforted by others' shame because it helps me feel less alone with my own shame. Maybe this is why they say that misery loves company. Maybe this is why Adam blamed Eve for his sin and Eve blamed the serpent for hers. Maybe this is why the Pharisees acted like bullies—why those hurting people went around hurting other people. Maybe they acted that way to help themselves feel less alone with their shame too.

The Healing of Shame

Before moving to Nashville to become the pastor of Christ Presbyterian Church, I got to spend five years learning from and serving alongside Dr. Timothy Keller at New York City's Redeemer Presbyterian Church. At the beginning of those five years, I felt privileged to be able to have Tim as a mentor and example. I especially felt privileged because I saw him as one of the strongest preachers and movement leaders in the world.

Even though I still feel the same about Tim as a preacher and movement leader, during those five years I grew to appreciate other things about him even more. Now, what I appreciate about Tim most is his love for Scripture, his deep prayer life, and his strong marriage to Kathy. And there is one more thing. Tim is the best example I have ever seen of someone who consistently covers with the gospel.

Never once did I see Tim tearing another person down to their face, on the Internet, or through gossip. Instead, he seemed to assume the good in people. He talked about how being forgiven and affirmed by Jesus frees us for this—for "catching people doing good" instead of looking for things to criticize or be offended by. Even when someone *had* done wrong or been in error, Tim would respond with humble restraint and self-reflection instead of venting negativity and criticism. As the grace of God does, he covered people's flaws and sins. Sometimes he covered *my* flaws and sins. He did this because that's what grace does; it reminds us that in Jesus we are shielded and protected from the worst things about ourselves. Because Jesus shields *us* like this, we should of all people be zealous to restore reputations versus destroying reputations, to protect a good name versus calling someone a name, to shut down gossip versus feeding gossip, to restore broken relationships versus begrudging broken people.

Tim could receive criticism, even criticism that was unfair, and it wouldn't wreck him. In his words and example, he taught me that getting defensive when criticized rarely, if ever, leads to healthy outcomes. He also taught me that our critics, including the ones who understand us the least, can be God's instruments to teach and humble us:

First, you should look to see if there is a kernel of truth in even the most exaggerated and unfair broadsides. . . . So even if the censure is partly or even largely mistaken, look for what you may indeed have done wrong. Perhaps you simply acted or spoke in a way that was not circumspect. Maybe the critic is partly right for the wrong reasons. Nevertheless, identify your own shortcomings, repent in your own heart before the Lord for what you can, and let that humble you. It will then be possible to learn from the criticism and stay gracious to the critic even if you have to disagree with what he or she has said.

If the criticism comes from someone who doesn't know you at all (and often this is the case on the Internet) it is possible that the criticism is completely unwarranted and profoundly mistaken. I am often pilloried not only for views I do have, but also even more often for views (and motives) that I do not hold at all. When that happens it is even easier to fall into a smugness and perhaps be tempted to laugh at how mistaken your critics are. "Pathetic . . ." you may be tempted to say. Don't do it. Even if there is not the slightest kernel of truth in what the critic says, you should not mock them in your thoughts. First, remind yourself of examples of your own mistakes, foolishness, and cluelessness in the past, times in which you really got something wrong. Second, pray for the critic, that he or she grows in grace.[7]

I've heard that the late Jack Miller had a similar response when people would criticize him. Out of a settled belief in the gospel, even when criticized unfairly by profoundly mistaken critics, he would softly mutter under his breath, "They don't know the half of it. I'm much worse than they think I am."

Author Brennan Manning once said, "Only reckless confidence in a Source greater than ourselves can empower us to forgive the wounds inflicted by others."[8] That same confidence can also empower us to stop inflicting wounds and to start catching people doing good instead.

The Source Brennan Manning was speaking of is the same Source drawn on by Tim Keller, Jack Miller, and millions of others who have tasted release from shaming and living ashamed. That Source is the voice of Jesus, properly amplified to drown out the voices of shame from outside and within. It's the voice that, having absorbed every bit of our shame on the cross, now declares to us:

> There is therefore now no condemnation for those
> who are in Christ Jesus . . . If God is for us, who
> can be against us? . . . Who shall bring any charge
> against God's elect? It is God who justifies. Who is to
> condemn? . . . Who shall separate us from the love of
> Christ? . . . For I am sure that neither death nor life,
> nor angels nor rulers, nor things present nor things to
> come, nor powers, nor height nor depth, nor anything
> else in all creation, will be able to separate us from the
> love of God in Christ Jesus our Lord.
>
> ROMANS 8:1, 31-39

Let's turn the volume up on this life-giving verdict of grace and freedom, shall we? Because when the volume goes up on this, the voices of shame can't help but be silenced.

— o —

SUMMARY: Shame is a powerful voice that leads us to believe wrong things about God, ourselves, and others. When the voice of Jesus is "turned up louder" than the voice of shame, we grow more humble and gracious, and we start to catch others doing good.

SCRIPTURE: Psalm 42:8-11; Romans 8:1-2, 31-39
There is therefore now no condemnation for those who are in Christ Jesus (Romans 8:1).

TO CONSIDER: How has shame been a part of your story? How has it shaped the way you think about God, others, and yourself? What are some practical ways that you can "turn up the volume" on the voice of Jesus that assures you that you are loved and that you belong?

Chapter Seven

BEFRIEND THE ONES YOU CAN'T CONTROL

NOT LONG AGO BOB BRADSHAW, the executive director and leader of staff culture at Christ Presbyterian Church, took us through a Myers-Briggs personality exercise. Part of the exercise was to identify well-known people from the past who shared our personality traits.

When it was time to discuss my personality (INFJ), which is apparently the most rare—accounting for less than 1 percent of people—we discovered that, according to the analysts, I share a personality type with two significant historical figures. The first is Jesus. The second is Adolf Hitler.

What the—?!

Sadly, it's not always Jesus that people see in me. Sometimes the Hitler in me—the controlling, intense, hardly-ever-satisfied-with-the-way-things-are part of me—comes out. And when he does, someone almost always feels hurt.

Fighting with My Wife and Child . . .
ABOUT THE BIBLE
After Patti and I got married, we decided to read from the Bible together every night before bedtime. To our surprise, the

experience wasn't nearly as positive as we had thought it would be, because our nightly Bible reading almost always ended in a fight.

We would start by opening the Bible to the night's reading. After reading, we would share insights. As a newly minted minister who took pride in his knowledge of the Bible, I was very confident in my own insights. Surely, my new bride would be impressed.

But Patti, being the inquisitive and thoughtful person that she is, would occasionally respond to my "brilliance" with a thought or two of her own. Sometimes as she shared, she would respectfully question my interpretation of the passage. "How do you know that's what it means?" she would sometimes ask. Instead of listening to my wife and accepting that in marriage, teaching and learning go in *both* directions, I would get defensive. Then Patti's feelings would get hurt. Then, wanting to regain control of the conversation, I would get upset with her for having hurt feelings. Then she would point out that I was acting like a self-righteous Pharisee. Then I would confirm her point by doubling down on how right I was about the Bible and how prideful *she* must be to question someone like me, because I had a master's degree in Bible.

Before completing our first month of marriage, we, the pastor and his wife, stopped reading the Bible together.

Several years later, while talking with our then six-year-old daughter about her Sunday school lesson, I again felt defensive about proving my biblical knowledge.

Recalling a lesson about King Saul, our daughter, Abby, said to us, "King Saul . . . I know who that is! That's the man who ran away when they wanted to make him king." I corrected her and said that actually, Saul wanted to be king really badly. She was mistaken, a sign that she needed to listen more closely to her Bible teachers. But she held her ground. And, once again, I tried to regain control of the conversation.

I asked, "Do you really think that you, a six-year-old, know more about the Bible than I do?"

Then I quietly slipped off into a room with a Bible, just to prove to myself that I was right—so that I could then go back and prove to *them* that I was right. Because if I'm right, then I will feel like I'm in control again—in control of the conversation, in control of the subject matter, in control of the people who should know better than to challenge a pastor about what's in the Bible. I turned to the story of Saul in 1 Samuel 10, and there it was. King Saul, hiding himself in the baggage because he did *not* want to be king (see 1 Samuel 10:22).

It's humbling to eat crow with your six-year-old regarding your supposed area of expertise. But that's what I ended up doing. Reluctantly, I apologized . . . and changed the subject.

From the Dinner Table to the Street

But that's not all. Recently, I was driving on a gorgeous fall day in Nashville. The leaves were changing color, the sun was shining, the air was at seventy-five degrees, and the top of my Jeep was down. But I missed all the beauty around me because I got fixated on a Corvette in front of me, not because the Corvette was a beautiful car (it was), but because the driver was going five miles per hour *below* the speed limit.

The nerve! Because I prefer to go five miles per hour *above* the speed limit, I got up close to his rear bumper, making hand gestures to signal him to let me pass, cursing the day that the slow-moving Corvette was manufactured and wishing a slower-moving, less sexy Yugo or Chevy Vega on its driver.

The comedian George Carlin said that there are two kinds of drivers on the road—the idiots and the maniacs. The idiots drive slower than you do, and the maniacs drive faster. By this definition, I am the maniac treating the Corvette driver like he is an idiot. Because just like I must have control over a conversation about the Bible, I must also have control of the road.

Gulp. Lord, why do I have to be this way? Why does my impulse have to be frustration and anger with others when they aren't doing it right? And by "doing it right," I mean centering their world on me. *Wretched man that I am . . .*

Having big feelings about small things, and then dumping those feelings on others. Trying to control conversations and control traffic. That's what we type A controllers do when we don't address our inner desire to lord over everything and everyone around us. That's what happens when we become right in our own eyes and then try to impose our rightness onto others.

But it backfires. In an effort to control, we lose control. In an effort to make people better according to *our* definition of better, we make people feel worse.

Our Own Worst Enemies

In the alarmingly appropriate words of the famous singer P!nk:

I'm a hazard to myself. Don't let me get me.[1]

And please, don't let me get you. If I hurt you, I want you to tell me, even if you are my daughter. *Especially* if you are my daughter, or a slow Corvette driver, or anyone else whose spirit has the potential to get hurt by my type A-ness.

Faithful are the wounds of friends who show me a mirror, who praise the good in me but who also point out what's hurtful, because such wounds are surgical, not punitive. Such wounds are restorative, not insulting. They call me away from the Hitler within and toward the Jesus within.

Thank God for honest family members, friends, colleagues, and even strangers. Thank God for you, Mr. Slow Corvette

Driver, for reminding me of the type A, driven, and hurtful maniac that I have the potential to be.

I want to apologize when I *need* to apologize.

And God knows, I want to change.

Now That the Kids Are Older . . . (Not Much Has Changed)

As I write this, Patti and I are preparing for the day when we will launch our Abby, now a high school senior, into adulthood. Four years later, we will also launch Ellie. Very soon, both of our daughters will go off to college and assume ownership of their lives.

College will represent a new milestone in which they will have fuller decision-making responsibility—decisions about what they do with their time, how much or how little they sleep, what and when they eat, whether or not they exercise, who they choose to socialize with and to date, the activities they get involved with, how much they do or do not study, and whether or not they become part of a church or a campus ministry or continue at all with the faith in which we raised them.

Sometimes this scares me. It feels vulnerable. And yet . . .

Abby is intelligent and an incredibly hardworking student. Her GPA is above a 4.0. She made the dean's list every single semester in high school and scored in the ninety-seventh percentile on the ACT. She is a highly sought-after babysitter because she is outstanding with children and always leaves the house in better shape than she found it. She pays for half of her gas and most of her clothes and recreation out of the money she has earned. She volunteers as a group leader for middle-school girls. She carves out time to live in community with people who have special needs. She traveled to China last summer to spend a week making vulnerable orphans smile.

Abby is globally minded, a product of her New York City

upbringing, and values the image of God not merely in terms of her own culture or tribe or economic position or politics or nationality or skin color, but based on the Bible's vision of one people under Christ from every nation, tribe, and tongue. Whatever she does in the future, she hopes to help make the world a little more just and a little less mean.

I'm proud of Abby, yet despite the hundreds of ways I can praise her, I struggle that I will soon be letting her go, releasing her into the hands of God more than ever before.

Mitch, the Pastor's Kid

My friend Mitch left Christianity when he left home for college. Mitch grew up in a home much like ours. Like our girls, he was a pastor's kid, active in youth group and regular in his church attendance. But when Mitch went off to college, he distanced himself from the things his parents had taught him, distanced himself from the Bible, distanced himself from church, distanced himself from Christianity, and distanced himself from Jesus.

When asked about what he believed, there was a time when Mitch would respond, "I don't know what I believe, but I do know one thing. I know that I hate Christianity."

Years later, Mitch is now a pastor to college students. Eventually he returned to the faith of his childhood, much more convinced about Jesus and the Scriptures than he had ever been before. But his path back to God and into the ministry included a prodigal season, one that no doubt had his parents up at night and on their knees regularly.

Once I asked Mitch why he thinks he strayed from his faith in the way that he did. His answer terrified me. He said, "I strayed because by the time I got out of high school, I was done with everything that looked, felt, or smelled like the world of growing up in a pastor's shadow."

Gulp. And yet, I understand.

When you are raised in a pastor's home, even if your parents do everything they can to normalize your childhood, your childhood is not normal. You are never just "Mitch." You are "Mitch, the pastor's kid," which means that almost every day of your life, you feel a disproportionate amount of pressure—whether other-imposed or self-imposed or both—to play the part of the "good kid" who is the example for everyone else's kids.

Upon occasion, our kids have also felt this pressure. One time, an adult pulled one of them aside and told her that because she is "the pastor's kid," she should be a good example to the other kids, "because people are watching." Though these words were well intended, they were not helpful. Such words communicate that a "pastor's kid" is a different breed of human, and is not allowed to just be a kid like everybody else. It's like Hester Prynne in Nathaniel Hawthorne's *The Scarlet Letter*, in which the town adulteress must wear the letter *A* on her chest whenever she goes out in public, as a reminder that she is the bad girl. Similarly, wearing the letters *PK* (Pastor's Kid) whenever you go out in public, as a reminder that you are supposed to be the good boy or girl, can be a hard calling. Because just like Hester Prynne, you live a disproportionate amount of your life in a fishbowl.

I long for my daughters to spread their own wings and develop identities that are unique and less tied to me and especially to my job. I'm excited for them to be able to live their stories outside the shadow and the nest. I pray that outside the shadow and the nest, they will be able to pursue faith on their own terms and at their own pace and as they do, grow to love Jesus more.

Bad Authors of Other People's Stories

It should be obvious, but it's also something that I am prone to resist: *the best fathers, like the best friends, recognize that God is the wisest Author of somebody else's story.* If we knew everything that God knows and if we saw everything that God sees about what is truly the best way for someone else's life to unfold, we would be less prone to judge and control.

And yet, when it comes to my children, sometimes I wish that I, not God, got to decide how their future stories would unfold and how their love for Jesus would grow. I want my kids to experience the current chapter of Mitch's story without having to go through the middle chapters. Honestly, there's a part of me that wants to coach God on how to write each chapter of their stories.

O me of little faith . . .

When it comes to the people we love most, controlling type A personalities like me need to remember that we are terrible authors of other people's stories. Only God is able to be the author and perfecter of their unique stories and their unique faith. He, not I, will complete the good work he has begun in them. And he will do this in his way, in his time, and through his chosen process for them. Their lives are in his hands, not mine. It is his sovereign care over the details and chapters of their stories that will get them where they need to be.

Their story is not mine to write.

It never has been.

I'm nervous about that, but I must surrender to it. It is hard for a controlling type A to surrender anything, especially the author rights to his own children's stories.

And yet, if their stories were to unfold in unexpected ways—having dreams go unfulfilled, experiencing loss, being broken-hearted, enduring a spiritual crisis—hope would not be lost, because God would still be in control of things. And it is always better for God to be in control of things than it is for us to be in control of things. Even for prodigals like Mitch, the prodigal experience became the trigger to resurrect in him an irrevocable, insatiable longing for Home.

How comforting it is to know that our children are just that—*Abba's children*—dearly beloved daughters of the covenant, held and kept by the one who alone is Father of us all.

— o —

SUMMARY: We often want to control the people and environment around us. But we make a mess of things when we try to play God. We are poor authors of other people's stories. The path to peace rests in relinquishing control to God.

SCRIPTURE: Philippians 1:6; Ephesians 4:20-23
I am sure of this, that he who began a good work in you will bring it to completion at the day of Jesus Christ (Philippians 1:6).

TO CONSIDER: Do you struggle with wanting to control other people? Where does the desire for control come from? Is it pride, fear, or both? What are some practical things you can do to both (a) take responsibility for loving those around you and (b) relinquish control over those same people?

Chapter Eight

BEFRIEND TRUE FRIENDS AND SIGNIFICANT OTHERS

MOST ROMANTIC RELATIONSHIPS begin with precisely that—a romance.

That was how it was when I first met my wife, Patti. In our dating days, I found her to be appealing in every way. She was intelligent, spiritual, sensitive, others-oriented, fun to be around, and easy on the eyes. Everything that mattered to me in a relationship, and especially in the person I would spend the rest of my life with, seemed to be beautifully combined in Patti. When I was with her, I didn't want our time together to end. When I was absent from her, I couldn't wait for the next opportunity to reconnect. Each time I arrived at her apartment to pick her up for a date, the song "Dream Weaver" would begin playing in my head. At least that's how I remember it.

Now, almost twenty-two years after our first date, and four cities, eight residences, five churches, two dogs, three goldfish, two hamsters, two teenage daughters, two miscarriages, two seasons of supporting each other through anxiety and depression, a brief season of unemployment, many road trips and medical procedures and doctor visits, not to mention a million offenses, apologies, and forgivenesses later, Patti is still all the things she was to me at the very start. But because of these experiences alongside her, my understanding of the true nature of romance has deepened significantly. I have come to believe that true romance is sustained not by strong feelings and active hormones as much as it is by the loyalty through thick and thin that comes from friendship.

In 2009, Arlie Hochschild of the *New York Times* released an essay called "The State of Families, Class and Culture." He observed that in modern times, we have a curiously consumeristic approach to love:

> On Internet sites and television shows, we watch potential partners searching "through the rack" of dozens of beauties or possible beaus. Some go on "speed dates"; others go to "eye-gazing parties"—two minutes per gaze, 15 gazes—to find that special someone. If advertisers first exploited the "restless spirit" by guiding consumers' attention to the next new thing, a market spirit now guides our search for the next new love. The culprit is not the absence of family values, I believe, but a continual state of unconscious immersion in a market turnover culture.[1]

According to Hochschild, many treat love *less* like a committed covenant and *more* like a cost/benefit proposition. In the modern West, where divorce rates are high and people delay marriage longer than ever before, love is often treated as a means to personal fulfillment and little else. As long as there is sexual and relational fulfillment, as long as we continue to enjoy one another's company, as long as our emotional connection comes naturally and we don't have to work for it, as long as we both feel that this relationship benefits us more than it costs us, we will keep going.

But as soon as one or more of these things changes, we hit eject.

Love is in crisis these days. Whenever "as long as we both shall live" is replaced with "as long as our loving feelings shall last," love ceases to be love.

The biblical vision for love between men and women is deeply different. Love's starting point is an others-serving orientation versus a self-serving orientation. Words like *love, covenant, submit, sacrifice, serve, feed, nurture,* and *respect* are freely used in Scripture to describe God's vision for his two image-bearers—male and female—coming together as one.[2]

These principles from Scripture also apply to nonromantic friendships. For Christians, the point and trajectory of marriage *and* friendship is the everlasting union between Christ and the church. Our goal, whether single or married, is to prepare ourselves, and also each other, for that union.

Naked and Unashamed

In the early chapters of Genesis, God describes how a man shall leave his parents and be united to his wife and the two will become one flesh. He also describes how Adam and Eve, the first and prototypical human couple, lived their lives before one another: "The man and his wife were both naked and were not ashamed" (Genesis 2:25).

They were completely exposed *and* comprehensively loved.

They were fully known *and* not rejected.

Naked and *not* ashamed. This is the ideal for marriage and all other human relationships.

This "naked and not ashamed" dynamic sets the tone for redemptive exposure between persons. In Ephesians 5, we are told that marriage includes a "washing of water with the word" for the purpose of one party presenting the other to Jesus cleansed, purified, and made lovely—holy and without blemish (verse 26). Though husbands are to take the lead in this, both husband *and* wife become the best version of themselves by submitting *to one another* in these things.

One of the most overlooked benefits of love is how God works through it to mature us. Part of why he puts us in each other's lives is to create a tension in our lives, a redemptive pressure, that has potential to improve our character. If love and friendship aren't leading us to grow in the virtues of love, joy, peace, patience, kindness, goodness, faithfulness, gentleness, and self-control, then love and friendship are malfunctioning in some way.[3]

All of us need partners in life who know the whole truth about us, who recognize that our social media profiles, résumés, and best behaviors tell only part of our stories. All of us need people who know us as well in private as they know us in public. Because only those who know us up close can help us in the journey of becoming our truest, best selves.

I need you to call my bluff.

You need me to call your bluff too.

Physicians for the Soul

In his book *Dangerous Calling*, Paul Tripp tells of a time when he and his wife were getting along very poorly. At the time, he was a successful and beloved pastor to his congregation. In the eyes of the members of his church, he could do no wrong. But his home life told a different story, because with his family, and especially in his marriage, he was an angry man. Once, during a heated argument with his wife, he told her that she should be thankful because 95 percent of the women in their church would give anything to have a husband like him. To this, she responded that she was among the other 5 percent.[4]

Dr. Tripp would later say that this response from his wife, words that cut him deeply in the moment, worked more like a scalpel than a sword for him. They became words that healed him instead of crushing him, that restored him instead of destroying him. The "faithful wounds" of her words became a turning point in their marriage, one that would trigger a sorrow and repentance over the angry man that he had become, and that would set a course for him to become a better, more gentle version of himself.

Like Paul Tripp, all of us need our covers blown at times. Otherwise we will never feel pressed to deal with the spots, wrinkles, and blemishes in our character.

I have certainly needed the same. This is one of the many reasons that I'm thankful for Patti. Through twenty years of marriage, time and time again she has nudged me back toward health when I have believed my fears over God's promises, clung to money and other false securities, dropped names to feel more important, worked too hard and rested too little, been a million miles away while sitting at the dinner table, responded to stress and disappointment with hurtful intensity, and become a different person in public than the person I was in private. Without Patti there to confront these illnesses in me as with a surgeon's scalpel, who knows how my character would have languished over the years? Her gentle refusal to let me get away with being less than the man God has created me to be has been part of God's process of completing me.

Think about it this way. If you are married, there are only three people who have access to your private parts: you, your spouse, and your doctor. If you are wise, you allow your doctor to examine you and even to perform invasive procedures when necessary, to expose things in you that are sick. This is for your well-being and health.

If we welcome this kind of exposure for our bodies, why would we not also welcome the same for our character?

If we want healing for our souls, we ought to welcome all significant others—spouses, mentors, friends, and small groups—to be faithful partners in the healing process.

Choosing a Significant Other

I will not lie. In general, I am a fan of online dating sites. Although I didn't meet Patti this way, I know of many couples who did meet online and who now have healthy, fulfilling marriages. There's something to be said for a resource emphasizing compatibility in the areas of life that matter most to us—whether spiritual beliefs, personality type, number of children desired, career goals, or something else.

But there's one thing I don't like about online dating sites. The very first thing a user sees is a photograph. Whether on a website or at a party, many will instantly eliminate 90 percent of potentially great partners on the basis of looks and body type alone. We've all heard it before, and some of us have even said it: "He isn't the best-looking guy in the world, but at least he has a warm personality," or "She isn't what most people would call 'hot,' but at least she's really nice."

At least?

Scripture teaches that "beauty is fleeting" (Proverbs 31:30, NIV) and that God prefers the heart over external appearance (see 1 Samuel 16:7). However, in practice we often exchange substance for cosmetics, internal holiness for external hotness, spiritual fruit for eye candy, and the heart for outward appearance.

When we do this, we get it backward.

There are really just two questions wise people will ask *first* as they consider who their mate and closest friends in life will be:

First: Does being with this person motivate me to move toward Jesus?

Second: Is this person looking for me to motivate her or him toward Jesus?

Things like popularity and physical attractiveness may appeal to us for a time. But when seeking long-term friendship and romance, we really should be looking first for two things: an honest and humble heart and a well-worn Bible.

In a sexually charged, image-driven culture, these two essentials are easily forgotten.

Humble and Faithful > Hot and Sexy

Another important part of long-term relationships is the ability to feel *safe* when our fragility, incompleteness, sinful tendencies, and high maintenance habits are discovered by the other. We all need to feel confident that even when we are at our worst, we won't be abandoned.

In the Bible, when David and Jonathan made a friendship covenant together, they committed to each other for life (1 Samuel 18:3; 20). Likewise, when Scripture says that a husband and wife are united and cleave to each other, it means they have become willingly and permanently *glued* to each other. For better and for worse, in joy and in sorrow, in sickness and in health, when they are at their best and when they are at their worst, they are bonded together as long as they both shall live.

As a pastor, I have always encouraged engaged couples to use traditional vows instead of writing their own. Traditional vows don't focus on how the parties *feel* about each other in this moment. Instead, they focus on what the parties *promise to be* for each other during seasons when feelings, which come and go, weaken or fade.

As C. S. Lewis once said, true love is revealed when you stay committed to the other person during those seasons when you fall "out of like" with them. He writes:

> People get from books the idea that if you have married the right person you may expect to go on "being in

love" for ever. As a result, when they find they are not, they think this proves they have made a mistake and are entitled to a change—not realising that, when they have changed, the glamour will presently go out of the new love just as it went out of the old one.[5]

The film *A Beautiful Mind* beautifully demonstrates covenant faithfulness through thick and thin, even after the initial "glamor" of marriage wears off. It chronicles part of the life of John Nash, the Princeton mathematician and Nobel laureate who was also a paranoid schizophrenic. As the mental illness gets hold of him, Nash becomes increasingly troubled and difficult to live with.

During one scene, a friend asks his wife how she can stay in a marriage that is so difficult and in which the give/take dynamic is so one-sided. Her answer: in the darkest moments, she forces herself to remember the man she first married. Her memory of the man John had once been gives her the energy to continue loving him in his current state.[6]

Seeing as Jesus Sees, Loving as Jesus Loves

However, it's hard to find strength to love when the only good motivators are from the past (truth be told, in real life, Nash's marriage ended in divorce). Thankfully, in marriages and friendships between Christians, we can draw not only on the past, but on the future as well. Because in addition to past history, Jesus gives us a vision for what the person in front of us will one day be.

Falling in love biblically means seeing the person in front of us as an incomplete work in progress who will one day be made complete; a flawed sinner who will one day be made a perfect saint; a weak, wounded, sick, and sore creature who will one day be made happy, healthy, and whole. It means looking at a person in the good moments and the bad, knowing that Jesus, who began a good work in this person, will eventually complete that work. And the work will be glorious.[7]

Don't just fall in love with who they are now, God says to us.

With eyes of faith, fall in love with their future, fully redeemed, fearfully and wonderfully remade self.

Jesus invites us—especially when marriages and friendships get difficult—to see ourselves and each other as he sees us. Jesus sees us and knows us with an everlasting love, with a love that has saved us from ourselves and that guarantees our future perfection. In our present condition, Jesus sees us as the acorns that will become oak trees, the apple seeds that will become orchards, the caterpillars that will become butterflies, and the random cacophonies of words and notes that will become musical masterpieces.

> [I am] confident of this, that he who began a good
> work in you will carry it on to completion until the day
> of Christ Jesus. PHILIPPIANS 1:6, NIV

When Jesus finishes the good work he has begun in us, we will see why he loves us the way he does—with a love that will never leave or forsake us; with a love that is bigger and stronger than our spots, wrinkles, and blemishes; with a love that is stronger than death; with a love that will save us from the worst in ourselves. Jesus' love will transform us into the beauty that he intends to have and to hold, forever and always, as his bride.

In light of these things, no more consumeristic romances or friendships for us. Only covenant. Let's live by faith and love by faith.

For what Jesus has begun in us, Jesus will complete.

That's something worth committing to.

— o —

SUMMARY: God puts us in close, covenant relationships as part of our growth. He promises to finish the good work he has begun in us and to use marriage and close friendship in the process. This is why we stay committed and don't give up on each other.

SCRIPTURE: Genesis 2:22-25; Philippians 1:6
Man looks on the outward appearance, but the LORD looks on the heart (1 Samuel 16:7).

TO CONSIDER: When it comes to choosing a close friend or significant other, what criteria do you use? Which matters most—physical appearance and pedigree or a humble heart and a well-worn Bible? Why is it important that the closest people to us also be given permission to challenge us where our character and Christlikeness is lacking?

Chapter Nine

BEFRIEND SEXUAL MINORITIES

THE CULTURAL LANDSCAPE is changing on the subject of sexuality.

The centuries-old, universal consensus among Christians, Jews, and Muslims—that God gave sex for marriage between one man and one woman—is being questioned not only by secular society, but within Christianity itself. Fading is the long-held belief that "immorality" and *porneia*—the New Testament Greek term for all sex that happens outside of marriage between one man and one woman—are the same thing. Western progressive Christians may say, "Ours is a different age." They conclude that biblical prohibitions about divorce, unmarried cohabitation, and same-sex relationships were written for situations unique to the time and setting but do not necessarily apply to our modern context.

Christians who find such new interpretations unpersuasive and biblically unsound are increasingly viewed as unenlightened at best and bigoted at worst. What are we to make of this new cultural landscape? Moreover, how *are* we to understand the Scriptures on this matter? And what are we to do with that understanding?

Have We Misinterpreted Scripture?

Many Christians are swift to distance themselves from a damaging, us-against-them posture on this issue. A condemning, shaming stance toward LGBTQ and/or unmarried, sexually active heterosexual men and women has proven to be hurtful and counterproductive. For some, forsaking a holier-than-thou posture has also included sympathy toward, and in some cases affirmation of, expressions of sexuality that have historically been seen as incongruent with faith.

As once–culturally taboo expressions of sexuality become mainstream, and as colleagues, friends, and family members "come out" with news of a pending no-fault divorce or a same-sex or cohabiting, heterosexual relationship, more and more Christians feel pressed to sympathize instead of condemn, to support instead of separate, to affirm instead of deny. To reinforce this instinct, sexual minorities are compared to oppressed minorities of the past, most notably the victims of slavery. The thinking goes like this: "Christians eventually shifted on slavery because they finally saw that slavery was biblically wrong. Isn't it time to make a similar shift with same-sex relationships? Aren't sexual minorities the new slaves, the new oppressed minority?"

This is a difficult leap, however, because every reference in the Bible about sex outside the marital union between one man and one woman is negative. Paul condemns the proslavery mind-set in his letter to Philemon, a slave owner who, according to Paul and the Holy Spirit, must stop treating Onesimus like a slave and receive him as a brother (see Philemon 1:8-22). The Bible has no parallel regarding sex and marriage.

As Scripture unfolds from Old Testament to New, it becomes

more progressive in the way it dignifies, empowers, and liberates women, ethnic minorities, the enslaved, and the oppressed.[1] At the same time, Scripture assumes a more conservative tone in the way it speaks of sex and marriage. For example, polygamy, a common marriage malpractice in the Old Testament, disappears by the time we get to the New. Starting with the Gospels, Jesus reaffirms that in the beginning, "God made them male and female . . . and the two [male and female] will become one flesh" (Mark 10:6-8, NIV). Qualified elders must be either unmarried and chaste, like the apostle Paul and Jesus, or monogamous (1 Timothy 3:2). When Jesus *refuses to condemn* a woman caught in adultery, he tells her to leave her life of sin (John 8:1-11). Her personhood is too sacred, her body too precious, for her to continue as an adulteress. In other words, unlike the liberation of slaves spoken of in Philemon, there is no place in Scripture that pronounces liberation for those wishing to pursue sexual relationships, including committed and monogamous ones, outside of the male-female marital union.

This teaching is unpopular in our late modern times. Yet if the true relevance of Scripture is that Scripture shows no interest in being relevant—that is, that it shows no interest in being adapted, revised, or censored in order to be more in tune with the ever-shifting times—then the sex question is one that sincere believers have to wrestle with. We must remain countercultural where the culture and the truth are at odds with one another. This, and this alone, is what will make Christians truly relevant in the culture.

Compelled by the *love* of Christ, we must not withhold kindness or friendship from any person or people group, and we must not engage in any sort of us-against-them posturing. This in itself is countercultural in modern society.

Compelled by the *truth* of Christ, we must honor and obey the Creator's design—even when his design is countercultural and, at times, counterintuitive to us. His ways and his thoughts are higher than ours.

Affirming Sex (and Chastity)

Jesus, who was an unmarried celibate man tempted in every way just as we are, affirmed sex within the male-female marital union. He invented sex. Sex is not a no-no. It is not taboo. It is a gift that invites husbands and wives to taste Eden together—naked without shame, known and embraced, exposed and not rejected. Proverbs invites a husband to find satisfaction in his wife's breasts. Song of Solomon pictures a husband and wife admiring, reciting poetry over, and adventurously enjoying each other's naked bodies. Paul the apostle, also unmarried and celibate, says that except for short seasons dedicated to prayer, able-bodied married couples should have sex, and have it often. History will culminate in consummation between Jesus and his bride, the church—a "profound mystery" that every believer, married and unmarried, can anticipate in the new heaven and new earth.[2]

God is also concerned that sex not be distorted, abused, or turned into an idolatrous pseudo-savior. *Porneia*, the Greek umbrella word for sexual immorality, represents any departure from God's design of a male-female, two-becoming-one, marital union.

Why is the Bible seemingly so *liberating* about sex inside heterosexual marriage but so *limiting* for every other setting? I once heard Tim Keller say in a sermon that God put ethical guardrails around sex because sex is the most delightful and also the most dangerous of all human capacities. It is a transcendent, otherworldly experience. Sex works a lot like fire. On one hand, fire can warm and purify. On the other hand, if not contained properly and handled with care, it can burn, leave permanent scars, infect, and destroy. So it is with sex. I have seen this play out in scores of pastoral situations over the years. "There is a way that seems right to a man," says the sacred proverb, "but its end is the way to death" (Proverbs 14:12).

It is not just religious people who recognize this reality. For example, comedian Russell Brand said the following about pornography:

> Our attitudes toward sex have become warped and perverted and have deviated from its true function as an expression of love and a means for procreation. Because our acculturation, the way we've designed it and expressed it has become really, really confused. I heard a quote from a priest that said, 'Pornography is not a problem because it shows us too much; it's a problem because it shows us too little.' . . . I think what he's saying is that pornography reduces the spectacle of sex to a kind of abstracted physical act.

He goes on to express that porn is a drug, not good for him. It represents voyeurism, obsession with looking at women versus interacting with women, objectification, and fear of true intimacy. "Pornography is not something that I like. It's something that I haven't been able to make a long-term commitment to not looking at, and it's affecting my ability to relate to women, to relate to myself, my own sexuality, my own spirituality."[3]

A Way Forward—Especially for Christians

So what is the way forward on sexuality? I'm going to propose something a little bit out of the box. What if we Christians, especially those of us who still affirm the "graciously historic" Judeo-Christian sexual ethic as described above, concerned ourselves less with defending biblical marriage "out there" and focused more on nurturing biblical marriage "in here"?

Maybe we should start by conceding that the culture war has

been lost on this issue, a chief reason being that for a couple of decades the Christian witness, in its zeal for truth, mishandled the truth by forgetting about love. We should also embrace a new opportunity to set aside the failed moral majority posture and replace it with the more biblical, life-giving minority posture.

I want to propose that in relation to the LGBTQ community, Christians focus less on what makes us different and more on how friendship and respectful, spirited dialogue about ideas and differences can be developed. After all, whether heterosexual or LGBTQ or other, we are all part of the human community and are better served by kindness *across* differences than we are by hatred and distrust *because of* differences. As Martin Luther King Jr. aptly said, "Hate cannot drive out hate; only love can do that."

When such a vision is embraced, great things can happen. For example, evangelist Kevin Palau and Portland's gay mayor Sam Adams came together across differences, combining ideas and resources to serve Portland's less fortunate. In the end, both parties saw the experience as a win, not only for Portland, but for them personally. It also opened doors of conversation about Jesus, the gospel, and the Kingdom of God in ways that no public morality protest ever could.[4]

Former US Surgeon General C. Everett Koop, an evangelical Christian, became the world's foremost advocate to combat HIV/AIDS, which was then believed to be a disease that only affected gay men.

And there is Chris Stedman, who self-identifies as both "atheist" and "queer," and who wrote the following in an essay advocating for more friendship and collaboration between atheists and Christians:

The divide between Christians and atheists is deep.
. . . I'm dedicated to bridging that divide—to working

with other atheists, Christians, and people of all different beliefs and backgrounds on building a more cooperative world . . . to see a world in which people are able to have honest, challenging, and loving conversations across lines of difference.[5]

Can we envision this for ourselves?

Can we envision a world in which convictions are not abandoned but deeply kept, and that not *in spite* of those convictions but *because* of those convictions, friendships are made and honoring dialogue happens "across lines of difference"?

Can we see a way forward in which friendship and serving the common good become the *main* emphasis for the Christian and LGBTQ communities? If Jesus chose a Samaritan to be the hero of one of his parables, frequented tax collector parties, and hung around people whose sexuality, drinking habits, and religious beliefs contradicted his own, I think we can do better than we have thus far.[6]

It's not that ethics are unimportant. Ethics are very important. But we can't talk about ethics in a productive way without the necessary prerequisite of friendship.

So then, what if Christians put less energy into protesting LGBTQ values? What if, instead, we channeled these energies in the same way C. Everett Koop did, to address things that plague the LGBTQ community the most—things like depression, self-hatred, isolation, bullying, estrangement from family, and disproportionate rates of teen suicide? The life-giving minority approach starts with the recognition that if Jesus loved and healed people alienated from the religious community, then so should we. If Jesus frequented both Pharisee *and* tax collector parties, then so should we. If Jesus affirmed the good he saw in a Samaritan, then so should we.[7]

And if Jesus—though deeply committed to historic biblical

sexuality—never scolded or protested against secular people for their damaged sexual ethics, *then neither should we.*

Instead of looking for new ways to protest against the sexual practices of our culture, what if we invested those same energies in creatively loving our neighbors as ourselves, and doing unto our neighbors—*all* our neighbors—as we would have them do unto us?

I don't know about you, but I'm ready to roll up my sleeves.

Madeleine L'Engle says that we "draw people to Christ . . . by *showing* them a light that is so lovely that they want with all their hearts to know the source of it" (emphasis added).[8]

The *telling* of the light will backfire wherever there is no *showing* of the light.

A Light So Lovely

Rather than condemning "sex in the city," what if we concerned ourselves instead with being the "city on a hill" that Jesus intends for us to be?[9]

What if we affirmed along with the Bible that being unmarried and chaste (like Paul and Jesus) is a noble and fruitful calling? What if we affirmed along with Paul that being single, though less common, is still a "far better" calling than marriage because it frees single men and women to devote themselves fully to the Lord's concerns? And what if we got rid of the term "single" in our churches and embraced a renewed biblical vision for the church as a surrogate family where every person, married and divorced and single, hetero attracted and same-sex attracted, has access to spiritual friendships as deep as that of David and Jonathan, whose mutual accessibility, transparency, and loyalty rivaled the love between a man and a woman?[10]

What if, while continuing to affirm the historic Judeo-Christian sexual ethic, we sought thoughtful ways to help ease the burden and help minimize the loneliness of those for whom this biblical ethic is quite costly? Recently, I heard a same-sex-attracted, chaste-for-Jesus'-sake man say that without the prospect of having a "significant other" through marriage, he is depending on the church to *be* his significant other. A same-sex-attracted woman shared how a family in her church offered her a room in their house and a seat at their table—*for the rest of her life*—if that's what it takes to support her in her commitment to lifelong chastity and singleness.

Can we imagine these kinds of scenarios materializing in *our* lives and faith communities?

And what if we shifted our emphasis toward the marriage of which all other marriages are but a shadow—the mystical union between Jesus and his bride, the church, which is inclusive of believing husbands and wives as well as widows and widowers, divorcees, and other unmarried men and women? According to sacred Scripture, no matter what one's marital status or sexual orientation, the first moment of trust in Jesus makes that person as married and complete as she or he will ever be. From our first moment of faith, Jesus is our bridegroom and we are his bride.

We are our beloved's, and our beloved is ours.

Finally, what if we focused on renewing marriage *inside* the church first, repenting of hard-core and soft-core pornography habits, taking captive the thoughts and fantasies that objectify other human beings, reducing divorces where biblical grounds do not exist, and nurturing love, lingering conversation, hand-holding, fidelity, and forgiveness and living face to face (in intimacy) and also side by side (on mission) within marriages? For unless and until we become *this* kind of countercultural community among ourselves—showing the light of Christ that is in us as well as telling it—any zeal for biblical marriage and chastity "out there" will fall on deaf ears.

And rightly so.

— o —

SUMMARY: God is pro-sex because he invented sex. Where the Bible prohibits sexual activity, Christians must take the lead in helping to ease the burden of loneliness because it is not good for anyone to be alone.

SCRIPTURE: Genesis 2:20-25; 1 Corinthians 5:1-13
For what have I to do with judging outsiders? Is it not those inside the church whom you are to judge? God judges those outside (1 Corinthians 5:12-13).

TO CONSIDER: Do you agree or disagree with how Christians have approached the public conversation about sexuality? Why do you think that Jesus never scolded people outside the church for their broken sexual ethics and practices? For those being told in Scripture to remain sexually chaste outside of the male-female marital union, how can the church help ease the burden of loneliness?

Chapter Ten

BEFRIEND DYSFUNCTIONAL FAMILY MEMBERS

FROM THE BEGINNING, the Bible speaks of family as a gift from God. When God creates Eve and gives her to Adam, Adam makes the poetic exclamation that she is "bone of [his] bones and flesh of [his] flesh" (Genesis 2:23). Even after the tragic rebellion with the forbidden fruit and the subsequent curse that infected all relationships as a result, family remains central to God's plan for flourishing societies and persons.

As it was in the beginning, so it still remains: it is *not good* to be alone.[1] As the poet John Donne famously said, "No man is an island."[2]

Being made in the image of a God who is both three and one, we are relational creatures by design. We need connection or we will languish. We need connection or we will wilt from loneliness and sorrow. God created the family as a key way to address this universal human need.

Family is the chief metaphor God uses to communicate how he wants to relate to us, and us to him. Marriage is a picture of Christ and the church. Children are a heritage from the Lord and pictures of God's Kingdom. Parents provide for, teach, and nurture their children and should be honored for this. God is our Father, and we are his children. He hovers over us like a protective mother hen. Jesus is both God and our elder brother who gave his life for us and is not ashamed of us.[3]

And yet, family is the source of many of our deepest wounds. Therapists probe patients with questions about family of origin. They do this because pain, loss, anger, alienation, co-dependency, and other forms of dysfunction are often conceived and cultivated within families. Resentments arise, fester, and develop when issues aren't addressed.

In the holiday classic *Christmas Vacation*, the main character, Clark Griswold, is alarmed when his high-maintenance cousin Eddie arrives unannounced for the holidays. In one scene, Clark's disdain for this lovable yet disheveled, aimless, train wreck of a man comes out this way:

"Eddie, can I refill your eggnog for you? Get you something to eat? Drive you out to the middle of nowhere and leave you for dead?"[4]

Why is this line so funny? It's funny because it's so relatable—this desire to experience relief, at whatever the cost, from family drama and those chiefly responsible for it.

Jesus' Own Family Was Dysfunctional

Even Jesus was impacted by family dysfunction. As large crowds were drawn to his teaching, his family wanted to seize him because they thought he was out of his mind. One time as he was teaching, someone came in and said that his mother and brothers were looking for him. To this he replied, "Who is my mother, and who are my brothers?" (Matthew 12:48). He would also say the following to his disciples:

Do you think that I have come to give peace on earth?
No, I tell you, but rather division. For from now on
in one house there will be five divided, three against
two and two against three. They will be divided, father
against son and son against father, mother against
daughter and daughter against mother, mother-in-
law against her daughter-in-law and daughter-in-law
against mother-in-law.   LUKE 12:51-53

Does Jesus oppose the nuclear family? Absolutely not! Rather
than take us out of our nuclear families, Jesus turns us toward
them—toward fathers, mothers, sons, daughters, sisters, brothers, and in-laws—as carriers of his love and care. And yet, Jesus
is saying that when the nuclear family falls out of sync with the
beliefs, mission, and ethics of the family of God, there are going
to be issues and tensions. But through the issues and tensions,
Jesus aims to work in and through his disciples for the redeem-
ing of fractured families and for the love of dysfunctional kin.
We see hints of this in the way Jesus relates to his own nuclear
family. Though they think he is out of his mind, he moves
toward them rather than rejecting them. As he is dying on the
cross, he entrusts his mother, Mary, to his close friend John.
James, his half-brother, later becomes a pastor in the Jerusalem
church and writer of a New Testament epistle.[5]

Speaking of Jesus' family, his declaration, "Who is my mother,
and who are my brothers?" would have caused offense. In those
days and times, family was everything—especially if, like Jesus,
you happened to be the oldest son. The oldest son was responsible for preserving the family name to the next generation, as
well as providing for and protecting the entire family . . . including the family's reputation.

What Jesus' apparent snub of his mother and brothers
does for us, however, is remind us that even for a perfect Son

like him, the nuclear family is a broken institution. As actress Mariel Hemingway is quoted as saying, "Everybody comes from pain and a certain amount of dysfunction." This is true even of Jesus.

Family dysfunction has many forms. Perhaps for Jesus' family, it was the embarrassment of having their son, also an untrained rabbi and carpenter and sometimes-homeless man, publicly put himself forth as the hope of the universe and only way to find peace with God. What's more, Jesus got up in the face of religious leaders, the pillars of Jewish society, and said that prostitutes and crooks were entering God's Kingdom faster than they were.[6]

Can you imagine the humiliation if this was your sibling . . . or even worse, your child?

If our sense of security, worth, and identity gets tied up in the behavior of a family member, heartache and alienation will surely find us along the way. And yet, when our anxiety escalates and our anger flares at a family member, it presents an opportunity to examine our own hearts.

Family: Wonderful Gift, Terrible Savior

What gives us our identity and happiness and value? If it's our families, then our families will wreck us, and we will wreck our families.

I have witnessed the joy of many weddings and also the tragic unraveling of some marriages. In my role as a minister, I am given a front-row seat in the most joyful and sorrowful moments in couples' lives. It is in the sorrowful moments, the ones in which romantic love becomes cold, and then hostile, and then irreconcilable, that molehills turn into mountains. The innocent mistakes of one spouse get labeled by the other as intentional; forgotten tasks as uncaring; fatigue as laziness; legitimate frustration as rage; constructive criticism as hurtful rejection; apologies as manipulation; and forgiveness as condescension.

But when motives are questioned and the benefit of the doubt is withheld, when a husband and wife are routinely irritated with each other, when humble apologies and kindhearted grace and forgiveness cease to be expressed in marriage, there's usually something deeper going on. It usually reveals that one or both spouses are demanding that the other be a savior, a true north, an *ultimate* source of happiness and fulfillment and meaning.

But as millions have discovered, anyone who looks to marriage to be *the answer* is going to end up lonelier inside marriage than living alone. It never turns out well when one broken sinner demands that another broken sinner be their Jesus. For only Jesus will never let his bride down. Only Jesus will never fail or disappoint. Only Jesus will know us fully and love us completely. Only Jesus will expose us but never reject us.

Similar sorrows emerge when children grow up with needy parents. Parenting out of neediness instead of love smothers children. Fearing that they will lose their children's affection, needy parents grasp for control. When control is denied, some will then punish verbally and even physically.

I once heard a counselor say that parents abuse their children not because they love their children too little, but because they love them too much. That is to say, if our "love" escalates into a need for or demand that our children think, believe, or behave in a certain way, the likelihood increases that we will melt down and punish when they inevitably fall short, instead of providing the safety and unconditional love that children need.

This is what you call reversing the flow of the umbilical cord: parents demanding that their children function as their source of life; their emotional nourishment; their identity; *their Jesus*. This always ends in sorrow and alienation and loss.

Just as in marriage, we must not place a burden on our children to provide for us the things that only God can supply.

What Family Can't Deliver, God Can

And yet, for those of us who have lived with family dysfunction or have caused dysfunction, there is greater grace that God extends to us. His mercies are new every day, and his offer to be our true Father, Brother, Husband, and Savior always stands.

What's more, if we have ears to hear and hearts to receive, God helps us feel less alone with the wounds inflicted by those who fail us. Even if we parent with grace and love, our children may grow disrespectful and unresponsive or go completely astray. If this happens, we have a God who understands. He is the perfect Father of children who are chronically ungrateful and unreceptive of his love.

If we have been scarred by Mom or Dad or both, God understands that, too. Jesus was the perfect Son who was misunderstood and was called a lunatic by his own mother. He was the perfect Son who was forsaken by his perfect Father—so that we, the prodigal sons and daughters who have been united with him by faith, would never be forsaken.

And, when marriage lets us down—when we grieve from unfulfilled longings to be married, or when we face loneliness inside a cold marriage—Jesus is the man who lived single and who died alone. He is also the loving, longing, faithful, and perfect husband who will never forsake his chronically adulterous, entitled, distant, unmoved, and always beloved bride.

In every family heartache, we have a Father, Brother, Husband, and Savior who is able to sympathize with our weakness because he has been tested in every way, yet is without sin or betrayal or infidelity or harshness or cold withdrawal or any other form of dysfunction.[7]

The Church: a Place of Reconciliation and Inclusion

Jesus gives us himself, and he gives us a family in the church. To disciples who had left everything to follow him, he responded with these words:

> Truly, I say to you, there is no one who has left house or brothers or sisters or mother or father or children or lands, for my sake and for the gospel, who will not receive a hundredfold now in this time, houses and brothers and sisters and mothers and children and lands, with persecutions, and in the age to come eternal life.
>
> MARK 10:29-30

Did you hear that? Who are your mother and father and sisters and brothers? Even if your nuclear family is a train wreck, if you are with Jesus then you have *another anchor family*— mothers, fathers, sisters, and brothers who, like you, are united to Jesus by faith. The church is God's redeemed society, a family of surrogates united together by one Lord, one faith, one baptism, and one God and Father of us all (see Ephesians 4:4-6). Sometimes this family, the Church, becomes a lifeline for those whose nuclear families are fractured or plagued with hurt and dysfunction. What's more, the Church can provide the support network, as well as relational, spiritual, and emotional resources, to enable Jesus' followers to move toward hurtful family members in grace, forgiveness, and hope. The Church can also provide wisdom and support for those who need to set boundaries with and perhaps retreat from nuclear family members due to destructive patterns of toxicity and/or abuse.

At its best, the Church can provide support and solidarity that transcends all other loyalties while also demolishing divisions. Peter, a loud and intense man, and John, a gentle and contemplative man, become as inseparable brothers through their shared union with Jesus. Simon, an anti-government zealot, and Matthew, a government-employed tax collector, are transformed from enemies to friends by that same union. David and Jonathan, the son of a shepherd and the son of a king, become the dearest of friends through a shared faith. These are merely a sampling of what theologian Donald Carson has said about the family of God:

> The church itself is not made up of natural "friends.". . . What binds us together is not common education, common race, common income levels, common politics, common nationality, common accents, common jobs, or anything else of that sort. Christians come together, not because they form a natural collocation, but because they have all been saved by Jesus Christ and owe him a common allegiance. In the light of this common allegiance, in light of the fact that they have all been loved by Jesus himself, they commit themselves to doing what he says—and he commands them to love one another. In this light, they are a band of natural enemies who love one another for Jesus' sake.[8]

This solidarity around the experience of loving Jesus—or, rather, *of being deeply loved by* Jesus—has also made the church the most inclusive community in the history of the world. This was felt deeply in first-century Jerusalem, where rabbis openly and often prayed, "Thank you, God, that I am not a woman, a slave, or a Gentile." In a culture of social pecking orders where Jewish men ran things and everybody else's role was to support them in their privileged position, Jesus came in to level the playing field and to reaffirm that all people are equal in dignity and value. The Holy Spirit then upended and negated the rabbis' prayers, arranging history such that the first three Christian converts in Philippi included two women—Lydia, who hosted a congregation in her house, and a slave girl—and a Gentile prison guard.[9] The Holy Spirit would inspire the apostle Paul, once an anti-Gentile persecutor of Christians, to become Jesus' "apostle to the Gentiles" and to write these words about God's redeemed family, the church:

> There is neither Jew nor Greek, there is neither slave
> nor free, there is no male and female, for you are all
> one in Christ Jesus.   GALATIANS 3:28

In the church, God has given us a family where healing can occur from the dysfunctions and sorrows experienced outside the church. What many have been denied in the nuclear family—a loving spouse, supportive parents, honoring children—is there for us inside the family of God, as it was there for Jesus.

We must accept that like the nuclear family, the church will also live with dysfunction until Jesus returns. However, we can treat ourselves and others with hope instead of cynicism because we know that Jesus will complete the work he has begun in us, because we are *his* workmanship, because resurrection and new life are in our future. We can live in confidence that we are not yet what we will be. We can look at the caterpillar in front of us—whether in the mirror or face to face with another—and envision the butterfly. Jesus will soon present his family, the church, to himself as a radiant bride without spot, wrinkle, or blemish.

So then, what if the church became the *first place* that people went looking for family? What if the church were filled with unmarried people but had no "single" people, because unmarried people were as family to each other and surrogate brothers and sisters and mothers and fathers and sons and daughters to the rest of the church? What if the church were the place where no parent felt the burden of having to raise children alone and where every child had *hundreds* of mothers and fathers and grandmas and grandpas and aunts and uncles and big sisters and brothers? What if it were true that God sets the lonely in families? What if the church were the place where anyone in the world could find refuge and solace from the age-old malediction that it is not good to be alone? This is exactly what God intended for the church to be.

Furthermore, when we pursue the anchor family that God provides in the church, we will actually end up "cleaving" better to our earthly families. Because in the church, we are taught to know God as a Father who protects, defends, and provides, and as a mother hen who gathers us under sheltering wings. In the church, we are taught to know Jesus as a brother who is not ashamed of us and as a husband who repeatedly forgives us, empowers us, holds us, and lays down his life for us. In the church, we are taught to know the Holy Spirit as a comforter, counselor, and guide. The more we come to know Father, Son, and Spirit in these ways, the more equipped, empowered, and energized we will be to protect, defend, provide, shelter, bless, forgive, empower, hold, lay down our lives, comfort, counsel, and guide in our nuclear families.

We might lose the desire to drive Cousin Eddie out to a secluded place and leave him for dead. Instead, we might start thinking creatively how we can love him well in his offensiveness and awkwardness.

Don't let your nuclear family be your Jesus. Instead, let Jesus and his family be your anchor family.

When you do, your nuclear family will be better for it.

— o —

SUMMARY: Prioritizing Jesus and his family, the church, serves the betterment and health of every other family.

SCRIPTURE: Matthew 12:46-50; Ephesians 5:21–6:4

This mystery is profound, and I am saying that [marriage] refers to Christ and the church (Ephesians 5:32).

TO CONSIDER: Why do you think therapists focus so much on the nuclear family when trying to help their patients? What is it about the nuclear family that impacts us, either positively or negatively, so much? Do you agree or disagree that placing priority on Jesus and the church can make us better members of our nuclear families? Describe your own experience in this regard.

Chapter Eleven

BEFRIEND THE CHILDREN

WHEN I WAS PREPARING in seminary to become a pastor, I was offered an internship at a local church. The pastor asked me what area of ministry I was interested in focusing on most. I told him I would do pretty much anything—teaching, adult discipleship, student ministry, missional living, worship and liturgy, or polishing the pastor's shoes and being his errand boy— whatever the church needed me to do would be fine. I told him that there was just one group I wasn't interested in working with—little children.

Looking back, maybe the pastor should have retracted the offer to give me an internship. But instead, he did me a favor.

Two days later, the pastor met with me to go over the terms of my internship. The first words out of his mouth were, "Scott, we have decided to assign you to the children's ministry."

I left the meeting feeling disrespected and not listened to. And yet, over the next couple of years serving in this internship, I realized that it was I, not the pastor, who had been disrespectful and had not been listening.

Now they were bringing even infants to [Jesus] that he might touch them. And when the disciples saw it, they rebuked them. But Jesus called them to him, saying, "Let the children come to me, and do not hinder them, for to such belongs the kingdom of God."

LUKE 18:15-16

C. S. Lewis once said, "I myself do not enjoy the society of small children. . . . I recognize this as a defect in myself."[1]

Do we recognize that an inability to enjoy children is not representative of a defect in the children, but of a defect in us? I hope that we do. And if not, I hope that we will.

Children offer us another unique opportunity to see what it means to live inside God's Kingdom.

Shifting Our Priorities

Like it or not, children are going to be who they are. With zero nuance or subtlety, they are going to be consistent—the authentic version of themselves—in every situation. Their raw honesty will come out in private as well as in public, at church or at restaurants, at bedtime and at breakfast.

It's usually very easy to know what children are feeling and thinking. It's easy to know where they stand. Sometimes it's incredibly messy. Children get hungry, angry, and "hangry." They get grumpy and tired. They have to go potty at some of the most inconvenient times and places. They can be disruptive, inefficient, and distracting.

But other times, children present us with a picture that is immensely beautiful, one that calls us back to *our* truest and best selves. Consider, for example, this reflection from my friend Gabe Lyons about his son Cade. Because Gabe's insights are true of children in general, I am replacing Cade's name with *children*:

[Children] pose a different kind of threat to society—
the in-your-face reminder that our aspirations for
"perfection" may be flawed. [Children] disrupt
normal. Whether it's [their] insistence that everyone
[they say] "hello" to . . . respond in-kind or [their]
unfiltered ability to hug a lonely, wheelchair-bound,
homeless man without hesitation: [children] bring
new dimension to what normal ought to be. . . . A
commitment to the common good demands we value
the elderly, the disabled, the unborn and those unlike
us. . . . We must allow life in our world that doesn't
follow our scripted narrative. We must have the courage
to choose that which is good over what is convenient.
. . . Would you be open to a new kind of perfection?
One that disrupts your current life, but that could
bring a deeper meaning you'd never imagined. . . .
[Children offer] an alternative view of the good
life. . . . They invite each of us to engage, instead of
simply walking by. They love unconditionally, asking
little in return beyond a simple acknowledgment.
They celebrate the little things in life, and displace
the stress that bogs most of us down. They seem to
understand what true life is about, more than many
of us. They offer us the opportunity to truly value all
people as created equal. . . . [Children change] us in
ways we would have never changed ourselves. [They
give] us permission to measure loving kindness over
productivity. [They offer] us a glimpse of God's grace
while shattering our preconceived ideas of what is most
important.[2]

Maybe this is why children scare us so much. Just like God,
they present us with a mixture of disruption and peace. But as

they do this, they bring us back to what our hearts know to be true: that in God's Kingdom, simplicity trumps sophistication, relationship trumps progress, and the least of these are the greatest. In short, all of the costs and inconveniences of love that children represent are *not* costs and inconveniences. Rather, they are God-given reminders of life as it's meant to be.

As Gabe reminds us, children mess with our "scripted narrative" of how life ought to unfold. But as they do, they become God's agents in our lives to change the narrative to a far better one. Children remind us that the greatest people in God's Kingdom—the greatest people in the world—are not those who "win" and get what they want and control things. No, the greatest people in the world are those who love and who serve. Children, perhaps more than anybody else, confront us with a fork in the road. Either we will take the selfish path, or we will follow children into the path of service. We will get about loving and serving.

Showing Us Ourselves, Showing Us the Father

One time Patti and I were both flattened by the flu. It was one of those illnesses that made it very difficult to get out of bed to do anything . . . and it held on for an entire week. On day three, one of our daughters entered our bedroom, woke Patti up, and boldly declared that her parents having the flu was unfair and it was getting really hard for *her*. Then she proceeded to invite Patti—her completely fatigued and flattened-out, flu-sacked mother—to rub her feet.

This bold and unfiltered honesty, this utter lack of situational awareness—it can be maddening, yes? And yet, as they say, the best way to measure your desire to serve is to look at how you respond when someone treats you like a servant.

By their honest example, children invite us to live authentically. They invite us to cry out and ask for comfort. They remind us that there is safety in being our real selves, that we need not be posers and actors hiding behind a mask. We are safe because we live every moment of our lives in the presence and beneath the gaze of a parent—of a good, good Father—whose love, approval, and favor can be assumed at all times.

This good, good Father never grows weary, and he never slumbers or sleeps. Our Father in heaven, who loves us *as* we are, loves us *where* we are—and also, like the best parents, refuses to allow us to stay there—this Father is there with his ever-faithful and healing reminder that we are at all times his beloved.

My father and my mother have forsaken me, but the Lord will take me in. PSALM 27:10

Can a woman forget her nursing child, that she should have no compassion on the son of her womb? Even these may forget, yet I will not forget you. Behold, I have engraved you on the palms of my hands.
ISAIAH 49:15-16

The older we get, the more cynical we tend to become. The more cynical we become, the less prone we are to believe that we are loved in this way, that we have this kind of access to the Father's care and reassurance, that we can cry out any time and for any need or desire to be met.

Even when we are wrongheaded and wronghearted, God hears and sees the true need beneath our awkward cries—the need to be seen, the need to be loved, the need to be reassured that we are never alone, the need to be remembered.

How long, O Lord? Will you forget me forever? . . . But I have trusted in your steadfast love; my heart shall rejoice in your salvation. I will sing to the Lord, because he has dealt bountifully with me. PSALM 13:1, 5-6

Children provide us with a necessary gut check. They challenge the distorted value systems that inhibit us from loving well. They are God-given reminders of life as it's meant to be.

Don't hinder the little children.

Let them come to me.

Jesus sweeping children up into his embrace is also an invitation—no, a command—to welcome them into ours as well.

The children will be the better for it.

And so will we.

— o —

SUMMARY: Just as children need us to raise them, we need the children to raise us also.

SCRIPTURE: Psalm 127:3-5; Luke 18:15-17

Jesus called them to him, saying, "Let the children come to me, and do not hinder them, for to such belongs the kingdom of God" (Luke 18:16).

TO CONSIDER: What bothers you most about small children? When tempted to avoid children or those who mess with our "scripted narratives," what opportunities do we miss to grow ourselves as children of God? What specific things can you do to encounter children more than you do currently?

Chapter Twelve

BEFRIEND THOSE GRIEVING AND DYING

AS I WRITE THIS CHAPTER, I am aware of the clock. In four hours, I will accompany my parents to Vanderbilt University Medical Center, where my mother will be examined by some of the best doctors in the world. Mom has been struggling with a later-in-life condition, one that serves as a cruel reminder of human mortality. As I watch her struggle, I am filled with sadness and anger, two emotions that are familiar to Jesus. Tears about Mom's situation remind me of the tears Jesus cried over the loss of his friend Lazarus. Anger about her illness reminds me of how Jesus got angry at death—that unwelcome, invasive guest in the garden of God that eventually gets us all.

As I watch my parents suffer together, I am deeply moved. All the temporal things that we tend to build our lives upon— the accumulation of wealth, material things, health, popularity, status, career success, and the like—fade into the background to a place of lesser gravity and significance. In their stead comes an awareness of the things that really matter: things like love, conversation, laughter, eye contact, holding hands to the very end, the treasuring of every moment, and tear ducts—the release valve that our weeping God created to help us exhale our grief. Tears are our stake in the ground, our tender yet tenacious protest against things like death, mourning, sorrow, and pain—things that we know intuitively are not supposed to be.

I am also deeply moved by my dad, whom I have always known as a person of stubborn strength. But his strength has taken on a new form these days, one that reveals something truly heroic in the man who, up until recently, I had never seen cry. Dad's tender tears over Mom are giving me a fresh glimpse into the nature of God. God, in whose image Dad has been created, is a God who weeps over things gone wrong in his world. He is a tender God who takes no pleasure in sorrow, suffering, or death. He is a God who comes alongside and assures us that he is here and that we are never alone. Moreover, he is a God who voluntarily suffered a death blow to save us from death's ultimate and final sting and to assure us that *he knows and has tasted* death and sorrow firsthand. As we face our mortality, we know that the immortal God did also. As we grieve the decline of those we love most deeply, we know that God did also. God buried a Son, after all.

These days, Dad is giving me a glimpse of this God and a front-row seat to observe what a real man looks like. Dad's tears are not a sign of weakness but strength. The vulnerability of tears and the admission of mortality that accompany those tears is a sign of true greatness.

Dad never leaves Mom's side these days. He is fully present with her, and he is fully present for her. His response to a struggling bride is to tell corny jokes that make her laugh. He holds her hand . . . *a lot*. He helps her with her hair and speaks tenderly, so tenderly, to her. These days, I catch myself looking at my dad and thinking, *This is the kind of man, the kind of husband, the kind of lover, that I want to be.*

His valiant tears, even more than his strength and successes, make me want to be a better man.

The Pastor I Want at My Deathbed

Pastor David Filson, who serves on our team at Christ Presbyterian Church in Nashville and is known by many as "Pastor David," is a remarkable human being. He is remarkable because of how he comes alongside people in their transition from this world into the next.

David does not avoid or run away from sorrow, grieving, and death. Instead, he moves *toward* these unwelcome enemies. He is always a first responder when people are in their most vulnerable moments. No one is more aware than David of the power that Jesus gives us to stare death in the face and say boldly, "You have no power over us. You have lost your sting. In the end, you will lose. In the end, you will be swallowed up, O death, by the one who conquered and defied you with an empty tomb" (see 1 Corinthians 15:54-55).

This is why David and I have made a deal that I will go first, because I want him to be the one singing hymns and reading psalms over my deathbed. I want him to be the one, after I breathe my last breath, who looks into the eyes of my wife and children and reminds them that death loses in the end, that resurrection is coming, and that we will all be eternally reunited with Jesus and each other. I want him to be the one to preach hope eternal at my funeral. Because no one preaches a funeral like David Filson does.

How did David become the death-defying man that he is? I believe the clear answer is that David has himself faced death many times. After a long battle with Alzheimer's, his father was welcomed into the presence of Jesus. After being temporarily defeated by cancer, his mother, too, was transitioned to paradise. In these kinds of moments, David weeps a flood of tears.

But through the tears he reminds his own soul that for the Christian, tears never get the final word. Like no one else I have known, David immerses himself in the scriptural truths—the written-in-blood guarantees that death, mourning, crying, and pain have no ultimate power over the story line for God's children. Death and sorrow are merely a middle chapter, a chapter that will resolve fully and finally when Jesus comes to make his blessings flow, far as the curse is found.

In the struggle against death, real hope cannot be found outside of Jesus. To face death without the risen Jesus in our corner, without the faith that alone enables us to grieve with hope, seems unimaginable. But for those who *do* trust in Jesus, for those whose lives *are* forever "hidden with Christ in God" (Colossians 3:3), there is an unshakable hope that will never perish, spoil, or fade away.

Christ has died,
Christ has risen,
Christ will come again.

The risen Christ has told us, "These words are trustworthy and true" (Revelation 21:5). These things are so because he *is* the resurrection and the life, and those who believe in him, even though they die, yet shall they live; everyone who believes in him shall never perish.

Dying and Grieving with Otherworldly Strength

I have had the privilege of walking closely with Christians in their final days. One such person was Billy.

Billy was thirty-five years old when he was diagnosed with terminal cancer. For a few short months, I watched this loving husband and father of two wither away from the disease that had taken residence inside his lungs. When Billy was close to the end, I went to his home for a pastoral visit, but he ended up pastoring me instead. "Scott, let's talk about you this time," he said. "How are you? How can I serve you? How can I be praying for you?"

There we sat, a dying man offering hope-filled prayers of love and life for his able-bodied pastor.

Soon after this, Billy died before my eyes. I will always remember that sacred moment. Friends and family, including his wife, Shannon, surrounded his bed and sang him into glory with hymns like "Great Is Thy Faithfulness" and "It Is Well with My Soul." This was their not-so-subtle way of defying death and stirring the imagination with reminders of what is true, even truer than the wreckage before their eyes. They were preaching the gospel to their own souls, reminding themselves and each other that there is a weight of glory that awaits them all—a weight that is so wonderful and certain that even the worst affliction will, in the end, seem light and momentary by comparison (see 2 Corinthians 4:16-17).

After Billy gave his final exhalation, I retreated to the waiting room. Here, I would sit and wait for Shannon to emerge. I anticipated all of the appropriate responses from this youthful widow—tears, anger, questioning God, and stress and sorrow about pending funeral logistics and raising two children alone. The emotional roller coaster would come to her eventually. But in that moment, Shannon became to me a sign from heaven. The first words she spoke as a grieving widow and single mother were, "Scott, how are *you* doing? Billy was your friend. How can I pray for you?"

As I walked to my car that day, I couldn't help but think how unworthy I was to know people like Billy and Shannon.

There are also others. I could tell you about John, whose body literally wasted away from ALS in two short years but who never grew cynical. Even on the hardest days, John was the most poised, prayerful, and hopeful person in the room. Jesus and God's promises of a new body and everlasting life, not his awful affliction, were John's ultimate reality.

I could also tell you about Steven and Mary Beth, who held a funeral for their young Maria—a horror that no parent should ever have to experience. Through their deepest sadness, these wounded warrior-heroes went on national television, along with their courageous children, to tell the whole world that death will not win. Because Jesus has risen and defeated death, there is a final chapter yet to be written in Maria's story—the chapter in which, as Steven has said in a song written in Maria's honor, "Beauty will rise! . . . Beauty will rise! And we will dance among the ruins; we will see Him with our own eyes!"[1] Also in Maria's honor, Steven and Mary Beth opened Maria's Big House of Hope, a place of refuge for Chinese orphans with special needs. Many of these children, like their Maria, will be adopted into permanent families through Show Hope, the nonprofit that they founded.

I could also tell you about David and Nancy, who lost not one child but two. Their Gabriel and Hope both died in infancy due to a rare congenital disease. Years later, the tears are still there, and the grief is still real. Like Steven and Mary Beth, David and Nancy are stewarding their tears in a way that brings hope to others. Each year they sponsor and lead a conference that brings comfort and hope to parents who, like them, have lost a child. Additionally, Nancy, a prolific author, has written several books that help thousands of people process their pain beneath the shelter of God's sovereign mercy and love.

Greatness through Sorrow

As I consider these and others who have shown faith, courage, others-centeredness, and even joy in the face of sorrow and death—most especially those I have gotten close to in friendship during their dying days—I have noticed a common theme that describes all of them.

They are all people who have, for years, leaned heavily on the Bible.

If you poke Pastor David with a fork, he will bleed Old and New Testament. When I asked Billy and John how they could live with such others-centeredness and otherworldly joy in their darkest hour, both said that they had read Scripture almost daily for years, and Scripture's promises had prepared them for the hardest days. David and Nancy, Steven and Mary Beth, and many others would agree: their refuge in the valley of the shadow of death is in God's Bible promises about the future of everything, including promises like this one:

> Behold, the dwelling place of God is with man. He will dwell with them, and they will be his people, and God himself will be with them as their God. He will wipe away every tear from their eyes, and death shall be no more, neither shall there be mourning, nor crying, nor pain anymore, for the former things have passed away. . . . Behold, I am making all things new.
>
> REVELATION 21:3-5

Those who lean heavily on the Bible are like the Olympic lifter who faithfully shows up at the gym every day for his work-out. The unseen, daily, faithful routine—the crunches, squats, bench and shoulder presses, the bicep curls—are his preparation for the day of heavy lifting when it finally comes. On that day, with all of his might, he lifts. He sweats, grunts, and groans with all of creation. At moments, he doubts he will be able to find the strength to press through. But in the end, he overcomes. In the end, he wins the gold.

For a Christian, the daily workout is one of mind and heart. Instead of treadmills, iron plates, and weight benches, her equipment consists of a receptive heart; a belief that God is sovereign, wise, and good; and a well-worn Bible. Her final piece of equipment is the doubter's prayer, the weighty prayer that must be "lifted" whenever she is tempted to follow her doubts and fears above what God has promised: *Lord, I believe! Help my unbelief!*

God's promise is breathtaking. C. S. Lewis sums it up this way: for believers in Jesus, heaven "will work backwards and turn even that agony into a glory."[2] Or, in the words of Lewis's close friend J. R. R. Tolkien, in the next world, everything sad is going to come untrue.[3]

Another person who knew this future reality well, and who believed it all the way down to her bones, was Kara Tippetts. Kara, wife of pastor Jason Tippetts and mother of four, died of breast cancer in her late thirties. She knew that her own death was imminent and wrote these words toward the end, which was also a glorious new beginning:

> My little body has grown tired of battle, and treatment
> is no longer helping. But what I see, what I know, what
> I have is Jesus. He has still given me breath, and with it
> I pray I would live well and fade well. By degrees doing
> both, living and dying, as I have moments left to live.
> I get to draw my people close, kiss them and tenderly
> speak love over their lives. I get to pray into eternity my
> hopes and fears. . . . I get to laugh and cry and wonder
> over Heaven. I do not feel like I have the courage for this
> journey, but I have Jesus—and He will provide. He has
> given me so much to be grateful for, and that gratitude,
> that wondering over His love, will cover us all. And it
> will carry us—carry us in ways we cannot comprehend.[4]

— o —

SUMMARY: Death, mourning, crying, and pain are difficult realities. Scripture's promises are our hope, both for future healing and present comfort. It is wise and good to move toward those who are grieving and dying as they lean on God's truth, both for their encouragement and our enrichment.

SCRIPTURE: John 11:17-44; Revelation 21:1-7
I am the resurrection and the life. Whoever believes in me, though he die, yet shall he live (John 11:25).

TO CONSIDER: Have you ever experienced suffering, sorrow, and/or death? How are you preparing your heart for that inevitable day when you or those you love will face death? Where does Jesus currently fit into your perspective about sickness, sorrow, pain, and death?

Chapter Thirteen

BEFRIEND THE POOR AND EMPTY-HANDED

ONE OF THE UGLIEST E-MAILS I have ever received came on a Sunday afternoon several years ago. Earlier that day, I had taught on how compassion for the poor was essential to faithful, biblical Christianity. The e-mail accused me of being a socialist, a Marxist, a left-wing radical, and unappreciative of those who "worked for a living." Apparently I had also failed to understand that poor people are poor because they are lazy. If they would stop milking the system, apply themselves, get educated, and go find a job like the rest of us, their problems would be solved and the world would be a better place.

As I read this e-mail, I felt anger. I'm pretty sure it was a good anger—the anger of Jesus rising up inside, a protective impulse for those he affectionately called "the least of these" and "heirs of the Kingdom" (Matthew 25:40, 45; James 2:5).

At best, a lack of concern for the poor reflects a blind spot. At worst, it reflects an arrogant dismissal of Jesus and *his* concern for the least of these. As we are drawn in by Jesus' compassion for us, we will also be drawn in to a life of compassion toward the poor.

[Jesus] unrolled the scroll and found the place where
it was written, "The Spirit of the Lord is upon me,
because he has anointed me to proclaim good news
to the poor. He has sent me to proclaim liberty to the
captives and recovering of sight to the blind, to set at
liberty those who are oppressed . . ." and he began to
say to them, "Today this Scripture has been fulfilled in
your hearing. . . ." When they heard these things, all in
the synagogue were filled with wrath.   LUKE 4:17-28

Instead of sending Jesus an e-mail, they made plans to throw
him off a cliff.

Like Your Own Flesh and Blood

I'm not sure what motivated the e-mail that I received that
Sunday, but I imagine that it was partly an aversion to high-
maintenance propositions. Compassion for the poor—like all
true forms of love—will be messy, costly, and inconvenient.
But sometimes things that are messy, costly, and inconvenient are the most worthwhile things. Jesus certainly thought
so. Who was it, after all, that Jesus received while others were
pushing them away? Who was it that Jesus said were the heirs
of the Kingdom? It was the messy, costly, and inconvenient
masterpieces—namely, little children and the poor.

Through the Old Testament prophets, Yahweh declares that
authentic faith fights injustice, liberates the oppressed, relieves
burdens, feeds the hungry, shelters the poor, and clothes the
naked. Moses says that if there are any poor among us, we
should be openhanded and give generously and never begrudgingly, and we should give until the need is met. James, the half
brother of Jesus, writes that religion that is true and that God
accepts is the kind that looks after widows and orphans in their
distress. Isaiah takes it a step further when he says that we all

owe a debt of love to the poor and are to treat the poor as our own flesh and blood. We are to treat the poor *as family*.

When family members are in distress, loving relatives step forward as the first responders. Loving relatives stay with those who are hurting or experiencing loss. Loving relatives reorganize their lives—schedules, finances, mindshare, and energy—to carefully and strategically position themselves to share the burdens carried by their disadvantaged members.

At minimum, then, if the family metaphor holds true, neighbor love calls for intentionality with time and resources to ensure that those who "have" are participating with Jesus in his mission of mercy and justice to those who "have not." Full hands must become emptier in order for empty hands to be filled. I am talking about a redistribution of wealth, power, privilege, and opportunity—but a redistribution that is voluntary, not forced. One that is an overflow of the heart, not coerced.

> All who believed . . . were selling their possessions and belongings and distributing the proceeds to all, as any had need. . . . No one said that any of the things that belonged to him was his own, but they had everything in common. . . . There was not a needy person among them. ACTS 2:44-45; 4:32-34

A Matter of the Heart

It is significant that Moses instructed Israel to give freely and *not begrudgingly* to the poor. Maybe what weighed heavily on Moses was similar to what weighed on me after I received the Sunday afternoon e-mail lambasting the poor. Why would anyone *begrudge* the poor, think poorly of the poor, or pass judgment on the poor, especially when Scripture assumes such a compassionate, sympathetic posture toward the poor?

For Christians, the chief reason is amnesia, a forgetfulness that whatever one's station—whether empty-handed or rich in cash—all are laid low and made equal at the foot of Jesus' cross. We are all beggars and Jesus, *only Jesus*, has the bread . . . because Jesus *is* the bread.

I wonder if it's also a combination of being naive and arrogant. We can be naive about the lives of people in whose shoes we have never walked. We can also grow arrogant about our own privilege, power, and wealth, somehow believing that we are who we are and where we are *solely* on the basis of our own tenacity and dedication and not at all because of the conditions into which we were born.

It is easy to overlook the fact that most privileged people were born into privilege. It is also easy to overlook the fact that most poor people were born into poverty.

Do we fault the poor for being poor? This is no different than faulting a person born with one leg for his inability to keep up with others who were born with two.

Here is an underappreciated reality about the poor who are often accused of being "lazy": many of the poor give up trying because of a *system*—a one-legged system into which they were born—a system that will not, and in many instances cannot, create opportunities for them to move forward, because the world is set up for people with two legs. Lack of resources, absentee parents, failing schools, and a scarcity of vocational on-ramps make it much easier to quit than to try. Seventy percent of those born in poverty never make it into the middle class. Many children born into poverty are, statistically speaking, two hundred times less likely to attend college than my children. College and career aren't even on the radar. For these children, the chief thing on the radar—whether materially or relationally—is *survival*.

If my children go to college, hard work will be part of what gets them there. So will the world of opportunity, resources, education, nurture, and privilege into which they were born. We simply must not underestimate this reality. So much of what we become is a result of the cards we were dealt in the first place. If you're born with four aces in your hand, your likelihood of winning the pot is much greater than that of those born with a pair of twos.

If from a place of superiority you are tempted to begrudge the poor, resist. It is not right to take credit for the two legs you were born with, or for the handful of aces that were dealt to you by someone else. Yes, you have to use those legs and play those cards in order to win, but you should only do so while thanking God for the advantages he has given you. God gave you those two legs and those four aces, just as he gave you food, shelter, clothing, a sharp mind, an education, and on-ramps into opportunity.

How might Jesus be calling you to use these things to help those born with one leg catch up to those born with two? Would he have you support a child from Compassion or World Vision or serve a nonprofit in your local community? Would he have you dive in with a local church that prioritizes mercy and justice? Or open your home and table to a few who don't have the same advantages you do? Or steer your workplace toward philanthropy, community service, or training, hiring, and promotion practices that create opportunity for those less fortunate? The possibilities are many, but one thing is sure. If you are with Jesus, he has a role for you to play. Jesus is the King with all the riches and power who did not shelter himself from human need. He moved toward the weak, disadvantaged, oppressed, and infirm. He moved toward the beggars and the little children and the ones with special needs. The more we are drawn to this Jesus, the more we, too, will be drawn to the poor. And as we are, perhaps to our surprise, we will see glimpses of Jesus in the faces of the poor.

As you did it to one of the least of these my brothers, you did it to me. MATTHEW 25:40

The Poor Don't Need Our Pity

While they do need our compassion, the poor do *not* need our pity. Woody Allen once humorously quipped that it's better to be rich than poor, if only for financial reasons. But if we pay close attention to Jesus, we will soon discover that Woody Allen couldn't have been more wrong.

Jesus said, "Blessed are the poor in spirit, for theirs is the kingdom of heaven" (Matthew 5:3).

Blessed is the Bible's equivalent to our word *happy*. How can this be?

It can be hard for us to accept that material prosperity doesn't guarantee happiness. According to a study published in the *New York Times* on happiness, when people's financial income grows, their happiness has a hard time keeping up with their income. The United States, one of the most affluent nations in the world and the global leader in commerce and consumption, ranks fifteenth in happiness. All of the fourteen higher-ranking nations are *less* materially prosperous than the United States. Said one researcher, "Even in a very miserable condition you can be very happy if you are grateful for small mercies. . . . If someone is starving and hungry and given two scraps of food a day, he can be very happy."[1]

I'll never forget being prayed for by Ray, a friend whose world is one of material poverty, homelessness, setbacks, and empty hands. Ray prayed that I—the pastor of the big church from Nashville, Tennessee, who writes books and has a blog and lives in a comfy house and has never been concerned about missing a meal and has always been able to pay his bills— would know the security of the Father's care, the smile of the Father's love, the freedom of the Father's grace, the intimacy of the Father's arms, the friendship of the Father's family, *and the abundance of the Father's provision.* Ray prayed as a man who, possessing close to nothing, possessed all things. He prayed as a man with empty hands but a full heart. He prayed as a man with abundant gratitude, as if he had a secret treasure stored up in a world that I had only heard and talked about but perhaps had not yet seen.

In that moment, I began to wonder which of us was really living large and which was living in scarcity. I began to wonder which of us was running with two legs and which of us was running with one. I began to wonder which of us was carrying the aces and which of us was carrying an empty hand.

As Martin Luther aptly said, "We are beggars, this is true."

This is true, because we are all the same.

— o —

SUMMARY: The closer we are to Jesus, the more we will move toward the poor. The more we move toward the poor, the closer we will be to Jesus.

SCRIPTURE: Isaiah 58:6-10; 61:1-4; Matthew 5:2-12
Blessed are the poor in spirit, for theirs is the kingdom of heaven (Matthew 5:3).

TO CONSIDER: How would you describe your current relationship with the poor? In what ways has today's teaching challenged you? In what ways can it strengthen your understanding of Jesus' love for you and others?

Chapter Fourteen

BEFRIEND THE OTHER RACE

I HAVE A CONFESSION TO MAKE. Not long ago, I was naive enough to believe that electing a black president would go a long way in solving the race problem. And yet, fifty years into the post–civil rights era, it has now become clear that we are not yet ready to call ourselves a post-racial people. I was painfully reminded of this when a friend sent me a *New York Times* essay written by George Yancy, a black philosophy professor at Emory University, called "Dear White America."

In his essay, Dr. Yancy laments the state of things for people of color in Western society. In his view, when the history books, the evening news, entertainment, business, education, politics, theology, and church cultures are shaped predominantly by the white perspective, people of color have little choice but to live under what he calls "the yoke of whiteness."[1]

To white Americans, the use of this phrase may seem unfair. The word *yoke* feels inflammatory because it hearkens back to the days of slavery. We in the modern West are against slavery and the racism that supported it, right? The public schools are racially integrated now. Lynching and mobs and violence are all now punishable by law. White ministers like me quote black thinkers such as Dr. Martin Luther King Jr. in our sermons. We read books and essays by John Perkins and Cornel West, and we speak out and tweet for racial equality. It is not uncommon for a white person to marry a person of color these days or to adopt a child of another race. Most white people would say that they deplore racism and are sickened by the shedding of black blood by white bigots. Our hearts hurt over black casualties in Selma, Ferguson, Charleston, New York City, and all other places where racial violence has occurred. Where there is injustice, most white Americans would say that they stand with the victims and against the perpetrators. But do people of color feel that these things are all true?

Though many of these things *are* true, we still have a race problem. How do we know this? We know this because the subject of race still hurts for many people of color. Dr. Yancy writes:

> Don't tell me about how many black friends you have. Don't tell me that you are married to someone of color. Don't tell me that you voted for Obama. Don't tell me that *I'm* the racist. Don't tell me that you don't see color. Don't tell me that I'm blaming whites for everything. To do so is to hide yet again. You may have never used the N-word in your life, you may hate the K.K.K., but that does not mean that you don't harbor racism and benefit from racism. After all, you are part of a system that allows you to walk into stores where you are not followed, where you get to go for a bank loan and your skin does not count against you, where you don't need to engage in "the talk" that black people and people of color must tell their children. . . . As you reap comfort from being white, we suffer for being black and people of color.[2]

Are We Listening to Each Other?

Ten years ago, Dr. Yancy's words would have bothered me. I might have even dismissed them as unfair and unreasonable. I would have assumed, wrongly, that his chief goal was to make white people feel guilty for being white.

But over time, and because of the courage and truthfulness of friends whose skin is darker than mine, my perspective has changed. These days, I find myself more sympathetic toward, and not offended by, words like the ones written by Dr. Yancy. Largely through friendship and a lot of personal mistakes along the way, I hope that I am growing in my understanding of the minority experience in the modern West.

The love, patience, and candor of black and Asian men and women in my life has given me a new set of ears for Dr. Yancy's outcry. When I listen to him, I do not see a chip on the shoulder, unfounded anger, guilt mongering, or some sort of "reverse racism." Rather, I see a man representing the minority voice, appropriately fatigued from feeling unseen, unheard, misunderstood, misjudged, and in many ways written off by a white majority.

Recently, a friend who is black shared an insight with me about people who riot (which, by the way, is not something unique to people of color). He said that rioting is a terrible and damaging thing, and yet it comes from feeling helpless in a system that dooms you, by virtue of your situation and the color of your skin, to being disadvantaged and overlooked. "Rioting," my friend said with tenderness and concern, "is helplessness acted out. It is trying to give a voice to something without a voice."

In describing the act of rioting this way, my friend put his finger on a widely known truth: *hurting people hurt people.* Ugly behavior can stem from being treated as ugly. Destructive behavior can stem from feeling destroyed. Dismissive behavior can stem from feeling dismissed. Diminishing behavior can stem from feeling diminished.

Pause here. Go back and reread the statement from Dr. Yancy.

Can you hear the pain in his words? Are you listening carefully to the alienation and marginalization and "otherness" that he feels?

Am I?

Stuff White People Like

There is a satirical website called *Stuff White People Like* that is written by and about white people. For the most part, it is a poke-fun-at-ourselves commentary on the blind spots and deficiencies of white culture. One section describes how white people "like" ethnic diversity:

> White people love ethnic diversity, but only as it relates to restaurants. Many white people . . . will spend hours talking about how great it is that they can get Sushi and Tacos on the same street. But then they send their kids to private school with other rich white kids, and live in neighborhoods like Santa Monica or Pacific Palisades. But it's important to note that white people do not like to be called out on this fact. If you run an ethnic restaurant you can be guaranteed repeat business and huge tips if you act like your white customers are adventurous and cultured for eating food that isn't sandwiches or pasta.[3]

As a white person, I can read a paragraph like this and laugh. But I wonder if such a paragraph, while poking fun at how misinformed white people can be about true diversity, rubs salt in the wound for a nonwhite reader?

The kind of "diversity" described above is more cosmetic

than real, more recreational than relational, more token than authentic. In fact, it is not true diversity, because it requires zero self-reflection or change from the ethnic majority. On the other hand, cosmetic, recreational, and token "diversity" is costly to minorities because it requires them to do all the bending, all the adjusting, all the adapting, all the sidelining and sacrificing of *their own* culture and heritage and uniqueness, to assimilate into a white world where things are done in the "white way."

One time I gave a sermon on diversity at Redeemer Presbyterian Church in New York City, where I was serving as a preaching pastor. At the time, Redeemer was about half white and half Asian. In my sermon, I said something that I thought would resonate with my Asian brothers and sisters and maybe even cause them to stand up and cheer. I said:

> The Kingdom of God is as diverse as humanity is diverse. God has called people to himself, and into his church, from every nation, tribe, and tongue. He has called us to be one body, with one Lord, one faith, and one baptism. Therefore, there should be no white church and no black church and no Asian church and no Latino church . . . because there is only *one* church.

As I said these words, I had no idea how much hurt they would cause.

Afterward, an African American friend approached me to give feedback. Looking at me with sorrow in his eyes, he said, "Brother, you don't get it." This felt jarring and left me wondering what I had done wrong. But sometimes, a simple and direct statement of fact is what's needed to get us listening.

Soon after this, an Asian friend approached me, also wanting to give feedback. He humbly and courageously offered the following (this is a paraphrase):

Scott, since your sermon yesterday, I have heard from several friends who, like me, are ethnic minorities. All of them, to one degree or another, felt hurt by your words. Many of them grew up in minority-specific churches and felt that you delegitimized those churches in your sermon. It felt like you were saying that those churches shouldn't even exist. Scott, I really believe that you meant well and that you sincerely value the diversity God desires for his church. But I'm afraid your sermon moved us backward instead of forward. In a white-dominated society, sometimes the only place that ethnic minorities can freely celebrate the beauty and uniqueness of their cultures, the only place that people of color are free to fully be themselves, is in churches where *their* ethnicity is the majority. Your words about ethnically diverse churches may be helpful for a white audience. But for ethnic minorities, your words reinforced the alienation that many of us feel in a white-led world and also in white-led churches. I'm afraid that your sermon added to, rather than taking away from, that feeling of alienation.

As this friend spoke these things, I felt thankful and sorrowful. I felt thankful because he had exposed a blind spot in me. He had given me a glimpse of my inability to understand the minority experience and of how much growing I have to do in the area of race.

I felt sorrowful because, in an attempt to build some bridges, I burned them instead.

Appreciating the Minority-Culture Voice

More recently, I was invited to participate in a national discussion on race. It was an all-day discussion, and there were about twenty people present. The group was about half white and half black and included authors, musicians, social workers, pastors, politicians, nonprofit leaders, and a Freedom Rider.

Although I was invited several times to contribute to the discussion, I stayed silent for most of the day. Instead of talking a lot, which is a preacher's natural default, I decided instead to listen and take a lot of notes. Here are some of the things we heard from our black friends. Rather, what I mean to say is, here are some of the things we heard from *our friends*:

> "Please don't call me your black friend. This kind of label actually reveals the poverty of our friendship. Not until I am seen as simply your *friend* will it start to feel like you regard me as your equal."

> "Imagine if the goal of your whole life was proving to white people, who have all the power, that you are not a threat because of the color of your skin."

> "I am a dark-skinned man married to a white woman. Our light-skinned children have a much easier 'race experience' than our dark-skinned children do, even though they share the same DNA."

> "White gentrification is taking over black neighborhoods in virtually every major city. Gentrification is when the *haves* displace the *have-nots* without regard for the have-nots."

> "White privilege is our institutional muscle memory. Privilege is when you can be successful without ever having to touch base with any other culture."

> "There seems to be a lot of fear among whites in today's climate. Fear of giving up privilege. Fear of listening more and of speaking less."

"Today's climate presents a unique opportunity for white Christian leaders to humble themselves, to learn, and to advocate for their brothers and sisters of color."

"Pain and lament aren't often taught in white evangelical books. Learning to deal with pain is a gift that people of color can give to white people."

"We never hear about the big scary white man, only the big scary black man."

"Race is not an 'issue' for people of color. For us, it's our *whole lives*."

"White friends, please recognize that love means engaging every part of the minority experience. It means entering into the pain of it with us."

"As a former Freedom Rider, I speak mostly to Caucasian groups. I'm rarely asked anymore to speak to African American groups. They have lost hope. They think, 'What's the point?'"

"As a black man, I don't need people feeling sorry for me. Help me believe I can be somebody. Raise the bar on me, don't coddle me."

What I am learning is how important it is for me as part of the majority to talk less and listen more to the minority voice. I'm starting to see that because I haven't lived the minority experience and because I have for all my life "reaped comfort from being white" in a white-dominated society, I should be quick to listen and slow to speak. I should presume less, offer fewer solutions, and ask a lot more questions. For only when I listen to the pain of the minority am I able to love across the lines of difference in ways that are helpful and not hurtful.

Racial Justice in the New Testament

The pain associated with cultural inequality, and also with minority versus majority dynamics, is not new. In fact, an overlooked minority was one of the earliest problems in the New Testament church.

The Christian church began with an all-Hebrew (Aramaic-speaking) leadership. However, it didn't take long before a complaint arose from Hellenist (Greek-speaking) minorities against the Hebrew majority, because the all-Hebrew leaders were not hearing the cries of the suffering, underserved, and overlooked Hellenist widows.

With all the privilege and power in their favor, the Hebrews had the luxury of not being required to respond. As the majority, they could have simply dismissed the concerns of the Hellenist minority rather than going through the trouble, inconvenience, costliness, and awkwardness of addressing their complaint. They could have easily responded to their Hellenist brothers and sisters, "Can't you just be grateful that we are allowing you to be part of our community? Don't you realize that it's not a very 'Christian' thing to complain? Why can't you just appreciate what you *do* have?"

Or they could have simply showed the offended Hellenists the door, sending them down the street, perhaps, to start a community of their own. "Since you're not happy here, since you don't seem to like our culture or the way that we are running things, then why don't you just go somewhere else and start your own church?"

In multiple ways, the Hebrew majority could have dismissed the minority complaint. But that's not what they did. Rather than responding defensively, rather than writing off the concerns of the minority, the all-Hebrew leaders handed the entire widow-care system over to the offended minority. Seven people were chosen to correct the issue of racial inequality in the church—Stephen, Philip, Prochorus, Nicanor, Timon, Parmenas, and Nicolaus—*all of whom were Hellenists.*[4]

You might say that the Hebrew leaders of the early church were among the first to take "affirmative action" to ensure that minority concerns were addressed and solutions were discovered and implemented by the members of the minorities themselves.

A first step toward true diversity—whether cultural, economic, political, ethnic, or otherwise—is to recognize that charity toward minorities by itself is not enough. Charity, to be truly charitable and biblical, must also result in empowerment, where the majority humbles and positions itself to *follow* the minority voice regularly. Especially where injustice and inequality exist, the majority must proactively seek out ways to surrender microphone and gavel rights to the minority. Invitations to give "input" must be replaced with opportunities to *lead*. Crumbs from the table must be replaced with a *seat* at the table. Otherwise, we remain stuck with an anemic, counterfeit diversity. Otherwise, particularly as pertains to race, we remain stuck with only stuff that white people like.

An Unexpected Invitation

My friend Pastor Ronnie Mitchell is more than a friend. He is also a mentor to me.

Pastor Ronnie calls me his "brother from another mother," and yet, we are different. He has lived in the same neighborhood his entire life. He is nearly two decades my senior and has been married to the same woman for almost as long as I have been alive. While also working a second job, he has pastored one African American congregation, New Livingstone Church, for close to forty years. He is also a black man.

In our time together, Pastor Ronnie has taught me more about life in Jesus than books or sermons have. He has opened my eyes to pain associated with being black in a white man's world, but never for a moment from a place of resentment or self-pity. In this, he has been to me a picture of grace and long-suffering. He has taught me how gentrification helps some while hurting others and how as neighborhoods get "better" for one people group, they tend to get worse—no longer accessible, that is—for another. He has shown me, in the presence of his granddaughter, what it looks like for a grown man to be wrapped around a little girl's finger. He has spoken twice at my church, both times bringing his whole church with him as a demonstration of unity and solidarity. In one breath, he is a model of dependent, childlike prayer. In the next breath, he shows what it looks like to storm the gates of heaven in power. Pastor Ronnie has taught me how sometimes the poorest people in the world are the ones at the top of the org charts and pecking orders, and the richest people are sometimes at the bottom. He has taught me, in ways that nobody else has, that the Kingdom of God is sometimes upside down to our sensibilities. And man, oh man, can Ronnie turn a phrase! But most important, when I'm close to Ronnie, I always sense that I am also close to Jesus. I need Pastor Ronnie for many reasons. I need him because in more ways than I can count, he makes me want to be a better man.

Recently, Pastor Ronnie honored me with an invitation to preach at New Livingstone's annual "revival." Before this, I had never preached at a revival. I had also never before preached to an African American congregation. But after the fact, I can confidently say that this was one of the top three most heartening experiences I have ever had as a minister.

From the moment I stepped foot into their sanctuary, the New Livingstone family received me not as a guest preacher but as one of their own. Their receptivity and hospitality toward me, toward the musicians from our church whom Pastor Ronnie invited to lead the singing, and toward our church members whom Ronnie invited to attend, was beyond welcoming. It was magnificent, a true taste of the Kingdom of God.

As I left full from that beautiful church that night, I wondered why Pastor Ronnie had decided to invite someone like me to preach at his church revival. Why would this pastor, whose community knows what it's like to suffer under "the yoke of whiteness," invite *me* into his pulpit? Why would he yield to *me* the sacred task of heralding a message of unity, love, reconciliation, and peace when the color of my skin, the zip code of my residence, and the history of my people in some ways represent the opposite of these things to *his* people? Why would Ronnie assume such a big risk for a leader in his shoes?

I think the answer is just that. The answer is that Ronnie *is* a leader.

For many years, Pastor Ronnie has taught his people, just as he teaches me, to see color not primarily through the eyes of cynicism and despair, but through the eyes of hope. He has taught his people, just as he teaches me, to see color not through the eyes of separation and alienation and otherness, but through the eyes of God's Kingdom reflected in *every* race, nation, tribe, and tongue. He has taught us all about how much we all need each other, to learn from and listen to each other and share life together, in order for the image of God to be more fully formed in us. By treating me as one of his people, as a brother from another mother who is on his team, Ronnie reminds me that being united to Jesus also means being united to each other. It means that through Jesus, our definition of "us" must expand, and our definition of "them" must shrink.

This is only part of why I lean on Pastor Ronnie, not only as a friend but a mentor. He is my mentor because he shows me what a real leader does in a racially fractured world. He did for me in his black-majority church what early church leaders did for the Hellenists in their Hebrew-majority church.

Pastor Ronnie handed the microphone of his black church to me, a white minister from the other side of town. He did not bring the gavel down on me; instead, he put his gavel in my hand. He did not treat me as a foreigner; instead, he treated me as a friend. He did not belittle me; instead, he elevated my dignity. He did not ignore me; instead, he treated me like I had something important to say. He did not caricature me as one of *them*; instead, he welcomed me as part of his *us*. He did not give me crumbs from his table; instead, he gave me a seat at his table. He did not call me a white man from the other side of town; instead, he called me his brother from another mother.

Pastor Ronnie is my mentor.

And from Pastor Ronnie, I still have a lot to learn.

— o —

SUMMARY: Throughout history and to the present day, racial tension has caused great pain, especially to ethnic minorities. However, for those with a heart to listen and learn, racial differences have potential to expand our vision for the Kingdom of God.

SCRIPTURE: Genesis 17:4-5; Galatians 3:28
There is neither Jew nor Greek . . . for you are all one in Christ Jesus (Galatians 3:28).

TO CONSIDER: In what ways has racial tension impacted your life and relationships? What have been your most difficult experiences in the area of race? What have been your most life-giving experiences? In what ways is it important for you to speak on the subject of race? In what ways is it important for you to listen?

Chapter Fifteeen

BEFRIEND THE RICH AND POWERFUL

WHEN OUR FAMILY MOVED to Nashville from an 850-square-foot New York City apartment, we had hoped for more living space . . . but not too much more. We had grown accustomed to smaller quarters, which drew us together and helped us live more simply. So we asked our realtor to find us a modest house within five miles of the church where I would serve as pastor. "Anything around 2,000 square feet will be plenty," we told him. But the smallest house he could find—the house where we now live—is almost twice that size.

Moving day would be the first glimpse that either of our daughters would have of our new home. When we arrived, our justice-driven, sensitive-to-global-poverty daughter exclaimed that the house was too much. Way too big. Enough room to fit *four families* comfortably. Why do we have so much space? This standard of living seems *wrong*. Although we didn't say it out loud, in some ways Patti and I felt the same.

There were two ironies that soon emerged from this moment. The first is that our 3,650-square-foot house ended up costing us about half of what the 850-square-foot New York apartment did. Second, within weeks, we all noticed that our *big* house was starting to feel *small* relative to some other homes we had visited.

Our former New York church and our Nashville church both have an unusual number of well-resourced and well-known people in the mix. This has forced us to wrestle with the question of wealth and fame. What does Jesus think about those who have money and celebrity? Is there a place for them at his table and in his circle of friends? Are others in our church— namely those living bankrupt or paycheck-to-paycheck—more virtuous because they have less? Is Jesus' imperative to the rich young ruler—that he must sell all he has and give it to the poor—nonnegotiable for *all* of his followers?

The Opulence of Jesus

> Mary therefore took a pound of expensive ointment . . .
> and anointed the feet of Jesus. . . . The house was filled
> with the fragrance of the perfume. But Judas . . . said,
> "Why was this ointment not sold for three hundred
> denarii and given to the poor?" JOHN 12:3-5

Despite Judas's protest, Jesus received the gift—a full year's wages worth of perfume—as he lounged comfortably at the table. This was the same Jesus who was born in a stall, died on a trash heap, and had no place to lay his head. This same Jesus enjoyed certain perks familiar only to corporate executives, preferred country club members, and blue bloods.

What's more, Jesus in his infinite wisdom—a wisdom that is sometimes perplexing and always greater than ours—has appointed some of his children to live poor and others to live rich.

Job, the most godly man on earth, was also the wealthiest.

Abraham prospered with land and cattle. Solomon asked God for wisdom and got wisdom *and* great wealth. Nicodemus and Joseph of Arimathea, both influential and moneyed men, secured a burial site for Jesus. Never once does Scripture condemn these and others for being rich. In fact, Scripture seems to say that "living large" is a feature of God's world untarnished by sin and corruption. History started in an extravagant paradise and will end in an extravagant city with many mansions, precious gems everywhere, and streets paved with gold.

Yet it's also true that . . .

Those who desire to be rich fall into temptation, into a snare, into many senseless and harmful desires that plunge people into ruin and destruction. For the love of money is a root of all kinds of evils.
I TIMOTHY 6:9-10

No one can serve two masters. . . . You cannot serve God and money. MATTHEW 6:24

Jesus told the rich young ruler, who was enamored with his wealth, that he would not be able to enter life until he sold everything and gave it to the poor.

Why would Jesus tell the rich ruler to give everything to the poor but not demand the same of Abraham or Job? It was because the rich ruler didn't really have money. *Money* had *him*. The man who thought he couldn't live without his money, in truth, wouldn't be able to live *with* it.

Scripture never says that having wealth is wrong, but *craving* and *serving* wealth is the problem. It never says that money is a root of all kinds of evils, but that the *love* of money is the real issue.

Compassion for the Rich?

The rich ruler chose money over Jesus. The idea of losing his upscale identity felt like too much to bear. But as the rich ruler ran into the arms of wealth, "Jesus looked at him and loved him" (Mark 10:21, NIV).

How could Jesus love this man who rejected him for money? A man who served his reputation and wallet above all else? Jesus was able to see past the greed to the fears and insecurities that drive the greed. Are we, too, able to look at the rich ruler *and love him*? Are we able to look at Zacchaeus, the wealthy, crooked, unjust, and friendless tax collector, and say, "We're coming to your house today; we want to eat with you, to be your friend" (see Luke 19:1-10)?

Why are anxiety and depression most prevalent among the rich? As Henry David Thoreau said, "The mass of men lead lives of quiet desperation."[1] This is the tragic biographical summary of many of the world's rich, who, in the poverty of their riches, have been plunged into ruin.

America's newly identified at-risk group is preteens and teens from affluent, well-educated families. In spite of their economic and social advantages, they experience among the highest rates of depression, substance abuse, anxiety disorders, somatic complaints, and unhappiness of any group of children. . . . As many as 22 percent of adolescent girls from financially comfortable families suffer from clinical depression. This is three times the national rate of depression for adolescent girls.[2]

Things are not always as they seem.

Jesus looked at the rich man overtaken with greed, *and Jesus loved him*.

Do we?

A Little Bit of Perspective

As I think about my own position, I really don't have any basis for indignation about the extravagance of others. As with every other thing, I need to examine my own situation and heart with thoughtfulness, care, and big doses of reality.

Here's the truth. Almost half of the world's population lives on less than $2.50 per day. This means that I spend more on coffee than many living image-bearers spend on their entire livelihoods. My family's little 850-square-foot New York apartment has a name to these image-bearers. Its name is *Palace*.

This isn't a cause for guilt. But it *is* a cause for perspective. In our standard of living, most of us are closer to the 1 percent than we are to nearly half of the world. What does this mean for us?

God wants his people in every place, not just some places. He wants his people among the rich as well as the poor. And so, in many instances, it is right and good—*a calling from God*—for some to live in the wealthiest neighborhoods, work at the wealthiest firms, have memberships at the wealthiest clubs, and run in the wealthiest circles. Why? Because the three-times-the-national-average depressed and suicidal preteens and teens from affluent, well-educated families—along with their moms and dads who are haunted in quiet desperation, as well as the executives, the celebrities, and the rich rulers—*also* need community with those who have found lasting riches in Jesus. How cruel would it be for the world's wealthy to be denied access to the embodied light of Jesus, who alone is the answer to the anxiety, depression, isolation, impossible expectations, mistrust of never knowing who true friends are, and fool's gold at the end of the rainbow that so many of the world's rich experience every single day?

Maybe the answer lies in the lyric from Si Kahn that was popularized by David Wilcox: "It's not just what you're given; it's what you do with what you've got."

Maybe the answer is in the high-ranking government official in our community, the one who uses his platform to fight for those without health care, who has so much integrity that the only thing his critics can say about him is that he is too nice, and who can regularly be found at fund-raisers for Young Life and global church planting. Maybe it's in the Grammy-winning artist and his wife who have invested their platform and royalties to found a nonprofit that makes it financially possible to place vulnerable orphans, many of them with special needs, into loving homes. Maybe it's in the writer who, when he discovered he was on a path to become a bestselling author, didn't dream about houses and cars and luxuries as much as he dreamed about joining C. S. Lewis and Rick Warren in the company of "reverse-tithers," those who donate *90 percent* of their wealth to the poor and to Kingdom causes. Maybe it's in the prolific, hall-of-fame songwriter who spends time with prisoners and college students and serves a church elder and who prefers quiet, faithful anonymity over fame. Maybe it's in the mom of six with a massive blog following who faithfully uses her platform to raise awareness and inspire action on behalf of the persecuted church. Maybe it's the rock star who has done similar things with his platform, the one who won't quit until all "stupid poverty"—the kind of poverty that can be eradicated—is indeed eradicated.

And maybe the answer is in the single, working mom faithfully doing what it takes each day to make ends meet. And the high school student who supports a Compassion child from her babysitting money. And the man who has lost his job and can't give a thing, but who thanks God for another day of food, shelter, clothing, and friends. And the twenty-two-year-old with Down syndrome who hands out bulletins at church.

It's not just what you're given; it's what you do with what you've got.

Jesus said something similar in his parable of the talents (a talent was a form of currency in Jesus' day). One man was given five talents, and another was given two. Both faithfully invested what they had been given and doubled their amounts over time. In the end, both received the same reward from their master; the one with four was just as much a contributor as the one with ten. Although their "net worth" was different, their worth in their master's eyes was the same. Both men were faithful with what they had been given.[3]

Having wealth and a platform are not special in themselves. As my wife, Patti, likes to say, "Everyone is a person of note, and everyone puts their pants on one leg at a time."

Said Job, the richest man of his time:

> Naked I came from my mother's womb, and naked shall I return. The LORD gave, and the LORD has taken away; blessed be the name of the LORD.   JOB 1:21

In the end, true wealth is about what Jesus has done to cover our nakedness. In the end, it's what *he* has done with the "talents" entrusted to him.

> [Jesus], being in very nature God, did not consider equality with God something to be used to his own advantage; rather, he made himself nothing.
> PHILIPPIANS 2:6-7, NIV

> Though he was rich, yet for your sake he became poor, so that you by his poverty might become rich.
> 2 CORINTHIANS 8:9

Maybe if we all started there—stripped of any illusion that we can be rich without Jesus—the *haves* and the *have-nots* could see how much we all need him and each other. Maybe we could see how, apart from Jesus, we are all poor in the truest sense. Maybe we could meet beneath his cross and, stirred by the love with which he has loved us all, bear each other's burdens—the unique burdens of having little, and the unique burdens of having much.

Because—rich or poor or somewhere in between—everything minus Jesus equals nothing.

And Jesus plus nothing equals everything.

— o —

SUMMARY: Everything minus Jesus equals nothing, and Jesus plus nothing equals everything.

SCRIPTURE: Job 1:20-22; Matthew 25:14-30
The Lord gave, and the Lord has taken away; blessed be the name of the Lord (Job 1:21).

TO CONSIDER: If we believed deep down that Jesus is our truest wealth, how would this impact our thoughts toward, and relational approach with, the haves in our lives? With the have-nots?

Chapter Sixteen

BEFRIEND THE BULLIES AND PERPETRATORS

ONCE I GOT REALLY ANGRY when I heard that a guy in prison had become a Christian. I got angry because I didn't think he deserved the blessings of God's grace, the comfort of God's love, or the assurance of God's forgiveness. And I certainly didn't think he should benefit from the promise of God's heaven. When I heard the news of this man's conversion to Christianity, for a brief moment I thought to myself, "I'd almost rather be damned than spend eternity with someone like *that*."

The man was Jeffrey Dahmer, also known as the Milwaukee Cannibal. In the course of thirteen years, Dahmer had dismembered and murdered seventeen men and boys. There are other unthinkable things that he did to his victims.

The news of Dahmer's conversion and my reaction to it pressed me to deal with the implications of my own Christian faith. If what the Bible says is true—that salvation is a grace that can reach *anyone* because it comes as a gift through faith in Jesus alone—then even someone like Jeffrey Dahmer is within the reach of God's forgiveness. Even a vicious, no-good serial killer can be made new by the scandal of God's kindness.

Truly, I say to you, the tax collectors and the prostitutes
go into the kingdom of God. MATTHEW 21:31

For by grace you have been saved through faith. And
this is not your own doing; it is the gift of God, not as
a result of works, so that no one may boast.
EPHESIANS 2:8-9

Face-to-Face with a Perpetrator

One Sunday after I preached a sermon on grace, a man named
Lou approached me. With self-hatred written all over him, Lou
asked boldly, "Pastor, do you *really* think there could be room
in Jesus' family for someone like *me*? It seems so impossible."

I responded by asking Lou about his story. He said he had
never told his story to anybody. He said, "What I'm about to
tell you is about a demon I created. It's a demon that I have,
ever since, carried with me. Others are carrying the demon too
. . . because of me. But first, can I ask again, could Jesus *really*
love *me*?"

My answer, this time more forcefully, was, "Of course. *Of
course* Jesus can love you. Take my word for it. If Jesus can love
me, he can love anybody."

I have to admit that for a moment, I would regret saying
these words.

Lou proceeded to tell me that he was a registered sex
offender. As he told me this, Patti and both of our daughters
were chatting merrily about ten feet behind him. I felt anger. I
felt confusion about Jesus and about grace. I felt protectiveness
toward my bride and daughters. Once again, the implications
of God's grace disturbed me deeply.

Then I remembered King David, the sex offender who
was also called the man after God's own heart. I remembered
Bathsheba, David's victim in more ways than one. David not

only took advantage of her, but then, to cover up the pregnancy that his sexual exploit had caused, arranged for the murder of her husband, Uriah. Bathsheba, by some great miracle of grace in her own heart, would later become the wife of David and mother of Jedidiah, whose name means "Beloved of the Lord." The other, primary name given to Jedidiah was Solomon, a name that means "Peace."[1]

> And David was the father of Solomon by the wife of
> Uriah. MATTHEW 1:6

Such stories are lovely, wonderful, and hope filled . . . until they become personal. I doubt that I'm the only one who has thought, in moments of gospel amnesia, that disgusting treatment of fellow humans should rule out and exclude a perpetrator from grace.

Grace is scandalous. Sometimes it's terribly offensive to our sensibilities.

And yet grace, by definition, offers hope to anyone—even the very worst.

Grace, though offensive when applied to *those people*, is the same grace for all of us. For without this grace, without a far-reaching grace, all people—prostitutes and Pharisees, moralists and deadbeats, victims and perpetrators—would be without hope.

At the end of the apostle Paul's life, he wrote a candid letter to his young protégé Timothy. In that letter, Paul wrote these words:

> I thank . . . Christ Jesus our Lord, because he judged
> me faithful, . . . though formerly I was a blasphemer,
> persecutor, and insolent opponent. But I received
> mercy . . . and the grace of our Lord overflowed for

me. . . . The saying is trustworthy and deserving of full acceptance, that Christ Jesus came into the world to save sinners, of whom I am the foremost. But I received mercy for this reason, that in me, as the foremost, Jesus Christ might display his perfect patience as an example to those who were to believe in him for eternal life.

1 TIMOTHY 1:12-16

Before Jesus saved Paul from himself, Paul had a different name: Saul of Tarsus. Saul, the aggressive persecutor; Saul, the violent bully; Saul, the insatiable killer who presided over the stoning of Stephen, the first Christian martyr; Saul, the man who, before Jesus stopped him in his tracks, was rushing toward Damascus to viciously slaughter more Christians.[2]

It's hard to believe that God used this bully resembling Hitler to write one-third of the New Testament, isn't it? It's hard to believe that through grace, Saul's violence was transformed to gentleness, his vitriol to tenderness, his sword to a healing salve, his racism to reconciliation, and his rage to love. It's hard to believe that eventually he, too, would be imprisoned and mercilessly executed for his faith in Jesus.

Believing Grace While Not Being Codependent

What does this mean for us? For the potential victims, the actual victims, and those who love the victims? For those who, like me, are nauseated by the bullies and the bullying?

One thing that it surely does *not* mean is that bullies and perpetrators get a free pass for bullying and perpetrating. Grace and forgiveness—whether granted by God or by people and whether granted to Jeffrey Dahmer or to Mother Teresa—are free.

But trust, and especially the vulnerability that comes with trust, must be earned.

Until then, be wise and maintain healthy boundaries with

those who have a track record of abusing and bullying and hurting people. This is precisely what the man Ananias did when the Holy Spirit announced that Saul of Tarsus was now Paul, and the former persecutor and violent man was now a chosen instrument to herald the message of grace, reconciliation, and peace.

> Ananias answered, "Lord, I have heard from many about this man, how much evil he has done to your saints at Jerusalem. And here he has authority . . . to bind all who call on your name." ACTS 9:13-14

It took a direct word from God for Ananias to move past his appropriate caution concerning Paul.

It also took fourteen years for Paul, who was formerly Saul of Tarsus, to learn the ways of grace and gain the trust of the Christian community, before he would begin his missionary journeys and letter-writing to the churches.[3]

In addition to caution, wherever there has been violence and injustice, anger by and on behalf of the victims is an appropriate—even godlike—response. About persecution and violence, the psalmist—also a victim of violence and abuse—writes:

> They band together against the life of the righteous and condemn the innocent to death. But the LORD has become my stronghold, and my God the rock of my refuge. He will bring back on them their iniquity and wipe them out for their wickedness; the LORD our God will wipe them out. PSALM 94:21-23

So then, there are really two possible "Christian" responses to a perpetrator:

On the one hand, if a perpetrator demonstrates no sorrow or

restitution for her or his abuses, the faithful response is to keep a safe personal distance while also confronting the evil by all means possible. Victims can also prayerfully celebrate that God, who will ultimately judge all and punish all evil, will achieve a complete and satisfying justice in due time.

On the other hand, if a perpetrator demonstrates proven sorrow—a sorrow that endures and that is accompanied by restitution, wherever possible, of what has been taken from the victims—she or he may be viewed as a candidate for grace. Jeffrey Dahmer and Lou, King David and the apostle Paul—each of these grieved over the thoughts, words, and deeds that introduced horror into the lives of their victims. In some cases, as in the case of King David, reconciliation was made possible through the forgiving grace of God. We see this played out in his epic prayer of sorrow and restoration, found in the fifty-first Psalm. David was reconciled to God against whom his adultery, murder, and abuse of power had been heinous sins. And Bathsheba—what an amazing woman she must have been—once David's victim, became David's wife and the mother of Solomon, whose name was *Peace*.

In the case of the victims of Jeffrey Dahmer and Lou, reconciliation may be neither possible nor realistic on this side of eternity. In such instances, the victims, and especially their loved ones who still feel the pain of their loss, must be remembered, prayed for, and shown heaps of compassion. May God grant them grace to forgive the perpetrators of their pain, not merely for the perpetrators' sake but for their own hearts and for their sanity's sake. May God grant them comfort to know that what makes no sense now will make more sense on the other side, where Jesus promises to make all things new and take away all death, mourning, crying, and pain.

As for those of us who have misgivings about the scandalous extent and reach of God's love? For those of us who need God's grace for ourselves but feel wounded by the grace God gives to certain others? Whatever wounds we carry, may we find solace in the justice of God—the God who will chase down vicious and unremorseful perpetrators and will, as the psalmist has written, wipe them out. May we also find solace in the grace that is so expansive that it has the power to reach anyone . . . even us.

The David and Saul in All of Us

Speaking of grace and perpetrators, I am compelled to quote a lyric from a song written by one of my favorite musicians, Sufjan Stevens.

In this particular song, Stevens hauntingly retells the story of John Wayne Gacy Jr., another mass murderer, who stored the bodies of his victims beneath the floorboards of his house.

The final words of the song are the ones that slay me most:

In my best behavior,
I am really just like him.
Look beneath the floorboards
for the secrets I have hid.[4]

These are the words that remind me that though I may be a victim, I, too, am a perpetrator. I, too, am a blasphemer, a persecutor, and a violent man.

Because it was my sins—right there alongside the sins of King David and Saul of Tarsus and Dahmer and Gacy and Lou—that put God's boy, God's Prince of *Peace*—on the cross.

God have mercy on us all.

— o —

SUMMARY: If God's grace can reach the likes of King David and Saul of Tarsus, then God's grace can reach anyone.

SCRIPTURE: Psalm 51; 1 Timothy 1:12-17

Christ Jesus came into the world to save sinners, of whom I am the foremost. But I received mercy (1 Timothy 1:15-16).

TO CONSIDER: Is there a type of person from whom you wish God would withhold his grace and forgiveness? What distinguishes this type of person from those you do want to see saved? If Jesus were standing in front of you, how would he minister to you in this struggle?

Chapter Seventeen

BEFRIEND VULNERABLE WOMEN AND HUMANS NOT YET BORN

I HAVE NEVER ENJOYED publicizing my thoughts about the pro-life vs. pro-choice debate. It's a heated issue. To take one side or another is to invite negative critique. Recently, as a courtesy to parents of young children, I announced to our church through e-mail that I would be speaking on this issue in a sermon. A variety of strong opinions about my sermon soon landed in my in-box . . . *before* I gave the sermon. I started to think that I would rather stay home and chew tinfoil than continue with this plan. *I am changing this sermon's subject to the evils of cannibalism*, I thought to myself. *Most people will agree with me on that one.*

I don't like stirring up a hornet's nest. I want people to like me.

But then I remembered my calling as a minister to teach the Word of God, whether in season or out of season, whether convenient or inconvenient, whether culturally engaging or culturally offensive. Teaching God's Word selectively would make me a charlatan at worst and a coward at best.

So I went ahead with it. But before doing so, I decided to

discuss the issue with several medical professionals, some on the pro-life side and others on the pro-choice side, including a handful of abortion providers. I thought it was only fair that if I was going to speak publicly on this issue, I should hear directly from all the perspectives. After listening to all sides and running each perspective through the purifying filter of Scripture, here are a few thoughts I would like to share.

The Core Issue
I believe that the core issue in the pro-life vs. pro-choice debate is whose rights matter most. Is it the rights of the mother or the rights of the infant in her womb? I believe that the answer is *yes*.

In his letter to the early church, James writes that we must show no partiality. He reiterates what Jesus said was the greatest commandment in relation to our fellow human beings—to love our neighbor as we love ourselves (see James 2:1, 8). In writing these words, James was addressing a problem that he saw in the first-century church. Favoritism was being shown to affluent, successful, famous people because everyone was trying to climb the social ladder. While the privileged were receiving VIP treatment in the church, the poor were overlooked. This, according to James, was wrong. In the church, every person is supposed to get the VIP treatment because every person, wealthy or poor, obscure or famous, strong or with special needs, mother or infant, is a carrier of the divine imprint. Every human bears the image of God. As Martin Luther King Jr. aptly said, "There are no gradations in the image of God. . . . God made us to live together as brothers [and sisters] and to respect the dignity and worth of every [hu]man."[1]

This is where the pro-life vs. pro-choice discussion breaks down. Though it would be unfair to label either side as being completely heartless and having zero compassion, *neither side is known broadly by the other for honoring the dignity of every human in the equation.* Now, I know many pro-life advocates who extend plenty of compassion and aid to both mothers and children through advocacy, orphan care, adoption, pro bono health care, and the like—but this narrative often gets lost in the politics and the shouting. Truth be told, neither side has made a compelling case to the other that is consistent with its own viewpoint.

Pro-life advocates allege that *pro-choice* is not an accurate term because only one person in the equation gets to choose the destiny of all people in the equation, namely the mother. She has 100 percent of the decision-making power, and the person inside of her has no decision-making power, no voice, and no ability to self-defend. The belief that all women should have jurisdiction over their own bodies also breaks down, because roughly 50 percent of infants in utero are females who have no choice over what happens to their bodies.

Conversely, pro-choice advocates allege that *pro-life* is not an accurate term. This is precisely the concern that an abortion provider once voiced to me. He said, "As I see it, the so-called pro-life position only applies to one kind of life. In my experience, after the infant is born, most pro-life people usually disappear from the picture." He went on to say that over 60 percent of women who come in for an abortion are alone and live in poverty. Many come to him under pressure from a husband or boyfriend—or even a parent—threatening abandonment if the pregnancy is not "taken care of." Though there are many valiant behind-the-scenes efforts made by pro-life advocates for mothers, rarely has this doctor *himself* seen or heard a "pro-life" person express concern for the pressures that tempt many mothers to make this tragic, irreversible choice.

And so it goes. Both sides are right in advocating for someone who is in a weak and distressed position. Both sides are wrong when they give preferential treatment toward one party and dismissive treatment toward the other. Neither seems to be fully in line with what James called "true religion," which is to attend to widows *and* orphans—to vulnerable women *and* children—in their affliction.

If we don't show deep concern for both mother *and* child, then our religion is lopsided. Until we become both/and on this issue, our religion is *not true*.

Is Abortion Equivalent to Murder?

Pro-life people focus on the ethics of pregnancy, namely the ethics of sexuality and human rights. When God's commands are ignored, injustices are bound to occur. James writes, "He who said, 'Do not commit adultery' also said 'Do not murder'" (James 2:11). Many pro-lifers would say that if people would stop committing adultery and murdering, the abortion problem would be solved.

This raises the question of whether or not terminating a pregnancy equates to murder. Can it be considered merciful in certain situations to terminate? Is there something to be said for sparing mother and child from public embarrassment, economic burden, disability, and other "problems" that can sometimes come with carrying a pregnancy to term?

Interestingly, two major Old Testament figures wrestled over this very question. Both struggled to believe that a difficult life was worth living.

Job was a victim of terror who lost all his assets, his business, his wife's respect, and all ten of his children. Jeremiah was a prophet in exile, hated by virtually everyone God had called him to love and serve.

Both men of God expressed the same sentiment: "Cursed be the day that I was born" (see Job 3:11, Jeremiah 20:14).

Jeremiah took the thought further when he said, "Cursed be the day . . . when my mother bore me. . . . Cursed be the man who brought the news to my father, . . . *because he did not kill me in the womb.* . . . Why did I come out of the womb to see toil and sorrow, and spend my days in shame?" (Jeremiah 20:14-18, emphasis added).

Someone on the pro-choice side might say, "See there? Even one of God's prophets said that he should have been aborted!" One might take Jeremiah's words to mean that he was in favor of the *quality-of-life* argument. If suffering is probable, says the quality-of-life argument, it is more merciful and just in some instances to terminate life rather than let it continue.

But if Jeremiah or Job truly believed this, each might have followed through with the thought and taken his own life. If the merciful and just thing to do with a life wrought by endless suffering and sorrow is to end the life and thereby end the suffering, why did neither of these men take their lives into their own hands? I think it is because in cursing the day they were born, both of these men of God were venting their raw emotions—emotions that were real but that were not necessarily based on truth.

In spite of expressing a desire to not go on living, many like Job and Jeremiah understand that the decisive issue is not the *quality* of life but the *value* of life.

Jeremiah did not take his life with his own hands, possibly because God had declared to him years before, "Before I formed you in the womb I knew you, and before you were born I consecrated you; I appointed you" (Jeremiah 1:5). Similar thoughts are expressed elsewhere in Scripture. "You formed my inward parts," the psalmist prays, "you knitted me together in my mother's womb. . . . Your eyes saw my unformed substance; in your book were written, every one of them, the days that were formed for me, when as yet there was none of them" (Psalm 139:13, 16). "He will be filled with the Holy Spirit, even from his mother's womb," an angel says about John the Baptist (Luke 1:15). The Old Testament Hebrew word used in reference to a toddler (*yeled*) is the same Old Testament Hebrew word used in reference to a fetus.

The Bible teaches unequivocally that from the moment that sperm and egg unite, you have a new living soul and carrier of the divine imprint. Personhood begins at conception.

People who believe the Bible are not the only ones who agree with this. The abortion provider I spoke with also said in the course of conversation that every abortion he has performed over the years has made him feel sick to his stomach. When his grandson with Down syndrome was born, he resolved that he would never abort a child with Down syndrome again. He also said that he believes human life begins at conception and that to terminate a pregnancy is to end a human life. While many—myself included—disagree with the doctor's willingness to perform abortions in spite of his beliefs about life in the womb, he deserves some credit for admitting that as long as he provides abortions, he will be morally inconsistent.

This is the moral challenge for those on the side of "choice." How is it possible, in the name of justice, to advocate for a woman's right to elect abortion, when the weakest human being in the equation is left without a choice and without a defense? Justice, to be truly just, demands that the most vulnerable, powerless, defenseless, and voiceless ones be entitled to and receive the strongest defense, advocacy, and protection.

As James writes, "Judgment is without mercy to one who has shown no mercy" (James 2:13). This is a weighty thing.

Do Pro-Lifers Protect Every Kind of Life?

Whereas pro-life people accuse pro-choice people of active aggression toward infants in the womb, pro-choice people accuse pro-life people of passive aggression toward mothers who are vulnerable.

Pro-life people must also grapple with the imperative to love our neighbor as ourselves. Otherwise we are fooling ourselves. Loving our neighbor calls for showing mercy. We may be pro-infant, but this does not necessarily mean that we are pro-life in the truest and most comprehensive sense of the term.

To show mercy is to lift a burden off afflicted people and take that burden on our own shoulders. Mercy puts itself in the shoes of those who are ashamed, alone, and scared. *What if it were us or our loved ones* who were faced with the realities of unexpected pregnancy? What if we were the pregnant, unmarried woman living below the poverty line? What if we were the college student who was a victim of date rape? What if we were the woman with a husband or a boyfriend demanding that we "take care of it, or else"? What if we were the teenage girl whose parents have made it clear that they will *not* support the birth or adoption route, but will *only* support termination, otherwise she is on her own? What if it were your sister or your daughter?

These are real situations.

A close friend of mine is a gynecologist who has never and will never perform an abortion and who is decidedly "pro-life." He relayed a real-time patient situation to me that seems as close to impossible as you can get. A young pregnant girl came to his office distressed. Why was she pregnant, and why was she distressed? Because a few thugs forced her into a private room and then, one after the other, took advantage of her ten-year-old body.

Yes, you read correctly. The girl was *ten*.

If you are pro-life, can you put yourself in the shoes of this girl or in the shoes of her parents and be satisfied with simply getting the law on your side for the sake of the child in utero? What about the other child who is carrying that child? Is it enough to vote your views and share your views on Facebook and put a pro-life bumper sticker on your car? Referencing

James again, is it enough for you to look at this ten-year-old girl and her parents and say, "You shall not murder. Now that we have that settled, go in peace, be warmed and filled. Take care of yourselves while I head off to the next picket line or political rally"—without giving them any of the things that they need?[2]

This is what the scribes and Pharisees were known for doing. They demanded that people keep God's law—don't commit adultery, don't murder, and so on—but they would not lift a finger to help share the burden.

A Way Forward

I believe that the only way forward is to adopt a Kingdom vision that transcends the civic vision on abortion. If we continue to hold the pro-life vs. pro-choice debate hostage by treating it as a merely political issue, we will get nowhere.

What might such a Kingdom vision look like?

The *Pax Romana* can teach us something about this. The *Pax Romana*, or "Roman Peace," was a term coined by the people in power during the first- and second-century Roman oppression. Social Darwinism was the rule of the day, and the terms of justice were decided by the powerful. This privileged class made certain that the terms of justice benefited *them*. The weak had no choice but to be subject to those terms. One historian described the *Pax Romana* as a coerced compliance in which all opponents had been beaten down and had lost the ability to resist and in which the weak and afflicted had no legal protection.

As in Hitler's Germany, certain classes of humans were seen as a drain on society and therefore disposable. Widows, the infirm, people with special needs, the poor, and unwanted children—all were vulnerable, and none had the assurance that their human rights would be honored.

Archaeologists discovered a letter written by a traveling Roman businessman to his pregnant wife. Unable to return home in time for the child's birth, he wrote to her that if the child were a boy, she should keep it. If it were a girl, she should throw it out.

In came the people of Jesus. Compelled by a Kingdom vision:

> No one said that any of the things that belonged to
> him was his own. . . . There was not a needy person
> among them, for as many as were owners of lands or
> houses sold them and brought the proceeds of what was
> sold . . . and it was distributed to each as any had need.
>
> ACTS 4:32-35

In ancient Rome, people of Jesus said to the Roman Caesar something similar to what Mother Teresa once said at a National Prayer Breakfast to a sitting US President: "Please don't kill the child. I want the child. Please give me the child."

By their care for those in distress, the early Christians said to the Roman Caesar, "We will take care of your sick. We will feed your hungry. We will shelter your widows. We will adopt and raise your children with special needs. We will take care of your pregnant mothers."

By the third century AD, the fabric of Roman society was transformed—"infected by love," as one historian has said. Even the Emperor Julian, known by history as "Julian the Apostate" because of his hatred of Christianity, conceded in a letter to his friend that the growth of the "Christian sect" had gotten out of control because the Christians took better care of Rome's afflicted than Rome did.[3]

What could this look like for us? I will leave you with an excerpt from a doctor who is a member of our church:

The centerpiece of our life and faith is the one who so loved us that he died for us. . . . Where does that leave us? First, don't murder. This is true for both sides of this issue. While exerting one's autonomy and taking of innocent life in abortion is clearly wrong and disallowed by Scripture, so is being vitriolic and hating others on the other side of an issue. Second, do unto others as you would want for them to do unto you—assuming your positions were reversed. Imagine that you are the one making a decision on the other side. As we fight about life in utero, let's not forget the person standing in front of us.

Build relationship and community. There is enough hurt to go around. . . . I believe that abortion is wrong. I believe that God is the giver of life. As a Christian, I want to support a society that does give preference to biblical ethics on this matter, because I believe that biblical ethics lead to human flourishing.

But wouldn't it be great if communities existed where *any* mother, married or unmarried, felt welcomed and loved and knew that her needs and the needs of her child would be attended to? If the Church everywhere does what the Church is called to do, then there will be no poor or disregarded or demeaned in our midst.

In short, I favor building community and dialogue that promotes a society where abortion, due to the love ready to be given to any child and any mother, is not merely illegal . . . but unthinkable.

— o —

SUMMARY: Being pro-woman and pro-child are two essential sides of the same coin.

SCRIPTURE: Psalm 139:13-14; James 1:27

Religion that is pure and undefiled before God, the Father, is this: to visit orphans and widows in their affliction (James 1:27).

TO CONSIDER: In the choice vs. life discussion, why do you think so many people prioritize a "pro-woman" stance over a "pro-infant" stance, or vice versa? What about the both/and approach being promoted here connects with you? What about it creates a struggle for you?

Chapter Eighteen

BEFRIEND STRANGERS AND REFUGEES

THIS WEEK I'M FEELING especially proud of the church that I get to serve as pastor. The people of Christ Presbyterian Church have a history of stunning generosity.

Being conservative in their theology—believing every word of Scripture to be right and true—our people are liberal in their loving. Being sojourners on the narrow path, they are people with a broad embrace. Believing Jesus to be the great physician and bearer of burdens, they have become healers and activists.

Over 30 percent of every dollar given to our church is sent out to mission partners in Nashville and across the globe, with special attention to the world's poor, marginalized, and oppressed. In 2010, a historic flood swamped our city. The members of our church, many of them suffering themselves, decided to set up shop to support and offer hospitality to others displaced by the disaster. Many opened their homes and their wallets to help shoulder the burdens of the people who were suffering most. If you attend any nonprofit fundraiser in Nashville—whether for fighting human slavery and sex trafficking, promoting the care of widows and orphans, feeding the hungry, advancing racial and class reconciliation, breathing new life into underserved neighborhoods and schools, or building on-ramps to meaningful work for the unemployed—you will find our people there, checkbooks in hand and eager to give. And they don't just show up at fundraisers to write a check; they also roll up their sleeves. Several hundred of our members engage regularly, some on a daily basis, in hands-on service throughout and beyond Nashville.

Love beyond Our Own Borders

Our world is facing the worst humanitarian crisis since World War II. For several years, men, women, and children have been fleeing their native land of Syria in fear for their lives. Close to sixteen million people are currently seeking refuge from vicious, life-threatening religious and sociopolitical persecution. Sadly, the Syrian crisis had gone under the radar in the West until ISIS started sending out videos of beheadings on beaches. Then a photo of a little boy, Aylan, dead on a beach, went viral.

When the picture of Aylan became public, many were appalled by the day's news but soon turned attention back to other concerns—more domestic ones—like a reality TV show billionaire running for president, a Kentucky clerk and some culture warriors holding a religious liberty rally with "Eye of the Tiger" bellowing in the background, Bruce being celebrated as Caitlyn at the ESPYS, Nicki calling Miley a name at the VMAs, Hillary's e-mail saga, and a fluctuating Dow Jones Industrial Average.

I hope that you will forgive the snarky tone of the last paragraph. I also hope you will find agreement with the irony represented there. How can we return so quickly to thinking *first* about these things when there are sixteen million souls seeking refuge and a cup of cold water in Jesus' name?

This is why I am proud of our church family. While some

of the above issues may be on their minds to a degree, *foremost* on their minds is their fellow humanity—sixteen million souls seeking refuge. This is their stance because they are keenly aware of what God has said about welcoming aliens and strangers and building cities of refuge for the vulnerable and how God so loved the world . . . the *whole* world:

> When a stranger sojourns with you in your land, you shall not do him wrong. You shall treat the stranger who sojourns with you as the native among you, and you shall love him as yourself, for you were strangers in the land of Egypt: I am the LORD your God.
> LEVITICUS 19:33-34

> For God so loved the [whole] world, that he gave his only Son . . . JOHN 3:16

Pastor and author J. D. Greear recently said on Twitter, "God builds his kingdom as we let go, not as we hold on."[1] This kind of "letting go" is what I have seen and experienced this past week. Our missional living staff sent out an e-mail to staff telling us that we *must* mobilize our people in the care of Syrian refugees. Very swiftly, our director of missional communities, Cammy Bethea, mobilized an effort that led to the formation of a one-stop how-you-can-get-involved web page, over $70,000 given and instantly deployed, partnerships with leading organizations on the ground, and an upcoming training session to equip people to provide sustained care for refugees. Nashville, a city of refuge in its own right, receives over a thousand refugees each year. All week long, people have been offering their homes, their finances, their time, and *their lives* . . . ready to do whatever it takes to get that cup of cold water into thirsty hands. Other churches are now joining the effort.

When local refugee relief leaders were asked how churches can get involved, they said people should follow the lead of Christ Presbyterian. It's amazing to watch a movement take shape.

God Bless America (and Everybody Else)

In the 2003 comedy film *Head of State*, Chris Rock plays the role of Mays Gilliam, an unlikely candidate for President of the United States. I have to admit that I remember very little about this film. The single thing I *do* remember, however, is the closing line of every campaign speech given by Gilliam's opponent, Vice President Brian Lewis: "God bless America, and no place else."[2]

We get the joke. The line represents the familiar caricature of a blowhard politician who will say anything, even senseless and ridiculous things, to pander for votes. Many of us will laugh off such an absurd line. And yet there may be others sincerely asking why we in America would want to focus on serving people from other lands such as Syria when we have so many concerns to deal with at home.

"Charity starts at home," some will say. On the one hand, it must start at home because if we are not taking care of ourselves then we are in no position to help others. And yet sometimes "Charity starts at home" is just a veiled way of saying that charity ends there too.

But Christians who appreciate that God so loved the *whole* world—Christians like Ken Leggett, Cammy Bethea, and others responding to the movement they have begun—understand that God is a global God who wants his people to love globally. Charity that starts and ends at home is not charity. It is short-sighted at best and self-absorbed at worst. But charity that starts at home and then moves outward—this is the kind of charity that causes heaven to rejoice. This is the kind of charity that honors the God of every nation, tribe, and tongue, the God who is for Jerusalem, Judea, Samaria, and the ends of the earth.

Recently, Patti and I were given the honor of sitting around a dinner table with a justice warrior, World Vision president, Rich Stearns. During that dinner, the subject of the Middle East came up, and he said something very provocative and also very *gospel*. With compassion in his eyes, he looked around the table and said, "What if, while ISIS was beheading Christians on the beach, just a couple of miles away Christians were feeding Syrian Muslims?"

With sixteen million souls out there seeking refuge, it seems that our time has come to consider Mr. Stearns's question. Our time has come to consider the hauntingly prophetic lyric from a band called the Brilliance:

> *When I look into the face of my enemy,*
> *I see my brother. . . .*
> *The wounds that bind all of humankind.*[3]

At the final judgment, Jesus the King will separate the sheep and the goats, the true believers and the religious posers. The true believers, having lived inside the King's immense love and experienced firsthand his generous welcome and hospitality, will have become hospitable lovers themselves. They will have been the ones who—in contributing to the welcome of alien and stranger, in participating in care for the least of these, in doing something big or small to provide food for the hungry and a drink for the thirsty and shelter for those without a home—will have welcomed King Jesus himself. "What you did for the least of these," Jesus will say, "you also did it for me."

Religious posers, on the other hand, will be exposed for a dead theology, for faith without accompanying deeds, for hearts and homes that offered no welcome, for charity that started at home and also ended there. The religious posers will have built borders around their hearts and lives, borders that kept things tidy and predictable and under control, borders that kept them safe from all the messiness and costs and inconveniences of love, borders that will show they may have never encountered the broad-reaching, transformative love of Jesus in the first place.

Not everyone is called to care directly for refugees. But every Christian *is* called—some in big ways and others small—to join Jesus in his declared mission to proclaim good news to the poor, announce liberty to captives, restore sight to the blind, and set at liberty those who are oppressed.[4]

The Activist Love of Jesus
for the Whole World—*Including Us*

When I read about the sheep and the goats, sometimes I feel more like a goat and a poser than I do a sheep and a true believer. Despite having been a Christian for twenty-six years and an ordained minister for seventeen, I am not yet what I should be. While over half the world is sick and dying from starvation, I overeat on a regular basis. While nearly half the world barely survives on less than $2.50 per day, relative to the rest of the world I have lived in luxury every single day of my life. While more than sixteen million souls battle the elements and long for a city of refuge, I live in an affluent, progressive, forward-moving "it" city in a neighborhood that is safe from danger and where there are two cars in every garage and a grill on every patio.

When guilt and a sense of not doing nearly enough kick in, I am reminded—so graciously—that it is not merely poor refugees who need rescue and shelter. It is also affluent refugees, ones like me, who need the rescue and shelter given by the Refugee-Savior who was poor.

Maybe Jesus cared so much about the alien, the stranger, and the refugee because Jesus was also an alien, a stranger, and a refugee. When he was born into the world, there was no room at the inn for him or his parents. Instead, an animal shelter, vulnerable to all the elements, became their refugee camp. And they were indeed refugees. Herod, the megalomaniac king, having heard the rumor that the Jewish Messiah had been born, ordered a decree for the slaughter of the innocents to purge the land of every newborn male. Mary and Joseph fled with their Jesus in search of other cities, homes, and hearts that had no borders.

It didn't end there for Jesus. After escaping from the murderous Herod, Jesus grew up, learning obedience through the things that he suffered. This included poverty and homelessness in his adult years. "The Son of Man has no place to lay his head," he said (Matthew 8:20). Having entered the world in a borrowed shelter, he would later feed his disciples at the Last Supper—also the first Lord's Supper—in a borrowed room. He would ride into town on a borrowed donkey, and then he would die and be laid in a borrowed tomb. He was the refugee who never found a home, washed up on the side of some lovely yet terribly vicious, murderous shore.

Why did Jesus endure such abuse? Why did he, being in very nature God, bring himself low, becoming obedient to the point of death? Because he was laser focused on bringing his banquet table not only to Jerusalem, but also to Judea, Samaria, and then—mercy of mercies—to us. Yes, we in the West are part of the ends of the earth.

We in the United States currently rank as the *most affluent* . . . and the *fifteenth happiest* . . . nation in the world.[5] Though we may not be running for our lives, many of us are living materially full lives and yet are spiritually, emotionally, and relationally running on empty. Many of us, here in the richest of all the nations, are among "the mass of men [who] lead lives of quiet desperation."[6]

We are refugees of another kind who, like the Syrians, need saving from the other side of the world. In different, yet no less desperate ways, we are helpless and homeless, in search of a city of refuge.

Enter the City of God, the City with no borders, the City that makes space and has prepared a room for refugees. These refugees may be rich or poor, others-centered or self-centered, overeaters or those who are starving, reality TV show billionaires or those running for dear life, famous or invisible, left leaning or right leaning, red or yellow or black or white, Syrian or American. Yes, the City of God has made room for us all.

Jesus is the poor man who sets a place at his table for the rich who are poor in spirit. Jesus is the homeless refugee who provides a home for those who are empty in their own homes. Jesus is the crucified carpenter from the little insignificant town of Nazareth who said to the affluent, influential jet-setters of Laodicea,

> You say, "I am rich, I have prospered, and I need nothing," not realizing that you are wretched, pitiable, poor, blind, and naked.   REVELATION 3:17

And his answer to this? Not a scolding but an invitation:

> Behold, I stand at the door and knock. If anyone hears my voice and opens the door, I will come in to him and eat with him, and he with me.   REVELATION 3:20

This is the same Jesus who said,

> Let not your hearts be troubled. Believe in God; believe also in me. In my Father's house are many rooms. If it

were not so, would I have told you that I go to prepare
a place for you? And if I go and prepare a place for
you, I will come again and will take you to myself, that
where I am you may be also.   JOHN 14:1-3

When Jesus promised to prepare a place for us, he made that
promise from the other side of the world. His are the words of
a first-century, Jewish, dark-skinned, never-married, physically
unimpressive and sometimes homeless, Middle-Eastern carpenter who never spoke a single word of English.

Why should we care about those in need on the other side
of the world who seem so different than us?

Because Jesus did first.

From the vantage point of Jesus of Nazareth, *we* are the ends
of the earth. And yet we are just as important to him as his
first twelve disciples. When *we* were hungry, he fed us. When
we were thirsty, he gave us something to drink. When *we* were
without a home, he went and prepared a place for us. When
we were withering on the vine and separated from the Vine,
he grafted us in. When *we* were living quiet lives of affluent
desperation, he welcomed us to his table for the poor in spirit.
When *we* were dying, he died in our place so we would live.
He became a refugee so we could lose our refugee status and
flourish in our forever home.

So let's roll up our sleeves and serve somebody, shall we?

— o —

SUMMARY: Our best reason for loving the whole world, and
not just our corner of it, is that we are "the ends of the earth"
that Jesus talked about. As Jesus saw, loved, and provided for
us, so shall we see, love, and provide for others in his great
commission.

SCRIPTURE: Genesis 17:4-5; Acts 1:8

You will be my witnesses in Jerusalem and in all Judea and Samaria, and to the end of the earth (Acts 1:8).

TO CONSIDER: How much would you say that God's love for the world—the *whole* world—plays into your own perspective? When you hear about how God reached to the ends of the earth to secure you for himself, does it overwhelm you or motivate you? What are your thoughts on the idea of charity starting at home and moving outward, versus starting and also ending at home?

Chapter Nineteen

BEFRIEND THOSE WHO VOTE AGAINST YOU

AS I WRITE THIS, the political landscape is heating up in the United States. Presidential campaigns are under way, and the airways are boiling with negativity and caricature—the tiring yet often expected strategies for winning elections.

Yet with each election cycle, as the mudslinging and caricatures escalate, I wonder if we have missed a marvelous opportunity that God has given us to actually change the world. Do you wonder this too?

Politics tend to stir emotions more than just about any subject. They bring out the best in us and also the worst. Like religion, politics can be polarizing and divisive, something we avoid at the dinner table. Partisans from the left and the right go to their corners, forgiving the weaknesses inherent in their own politics while being quick to point out weaknesses in the opposing view.

An election season is an opportunity for Christians to stand out as a thoughtful, fair-minded, and loving minority. To the degree that believers in Jesus can align with Jesus' approach to politics, the world will take notice. More important, the world will become a better place.

So then, what do the politics of Jesus look like?

There Is Only One True King

A band of secular and religious leaders try to trick Jesus with a question. "Is it lawful to pay taxes to Caesar, or not?" they ask (Mark 12:14). Then, they hand him a coin.

The inscription on the coin says, "Tiberius King, Son of the God Augustus Maximus, High Priest." With this inscription, the Roman emperor is claiming deity, and thus absolute authority, over all people in the empire. Rome was a totalitarian regime in which defectors, those who would not bow to the sovereign lordship of the state, would be executed on a cross.

Jesus gives an unexpected answer. He holds up the coin and asks, "Whose image is on this coin?"

"Caesar's," they reply.

"Well then, give to Caesar what belongs to Caesar, and to God what belongs to God."[1]

In other words, the coin is imprinted with Caesar's image, so the coin belongs to him. But *you*—all of you—are imprinted with God's image, so you belong to God. The coin is Caesar's, so give the coin up to him. You are God's, so give yourselves up to God.[2]

How brilliant. Not only does Jesus blunt the trap they set for him, but he establishes the proper ordering of things when it comes to kings and kingdoms. On the one hand, the citizens of God's Kingdom must endeavor to be the very best and most exemplary citizens of earthly kingdoms.[3] Even power-hungry leaders like Caesar should feel the positive ripple effect of Christian love toward people and places. On the other hand, none but God is entitled to absolute, unfettered loyalty. God alone is King, and his Kingdom is not of this world. When

God's Kingdom and earthly kingdoms collide, render yourselves unto God . . . and only to God.

Participation in Partisan Caricatures and Absolutes Is Patently Unchristian

If there ever was a partisan crowd in the Bible, it was the crowd of Mark 15—that famous chapter in which Pilate, so it appears, is entrusted with Jesus' fate. Here we find the crowd begging Pilate to release Barabbas, a political zealot, a murderer, and a purveyor of chaos. In his stead, they demand execution for Jesus. Jesus, who has been doing everything that a true revolutionary should—feeding the hungry, healing the sick, and sheltering the poor—must die. "Crucify him!" shouts the partisan crowd. Barabbas, the man of violence, is embraced as a freedom fighter. Jesus, the man of peace, is caricatured and crucified as an enemy of the state.

This is what partisans do. Partisans exaggerate the best features of their side and the worst features, real or contrived, of the opposing side. They minimize and overlook the weaknesses of their side, while dismissing the best features of the opposing side. What you end up with is someone being demonized and someone else being baptized by the crowds.

It's discouraging how easily we Christians can get drawn into partisan melodrama. How easy it is to participate in the politics of spin and caricature—ready and willing to tell half-truths to promote our candidates and tell more half-truths to demonize our opponents. Have we forgotten that a half-truth is the equivalent of a full lie? Bearing false testimony is always unbecoming of a follower of Jesus. It's one of the Ten.

If our politics lead us to believe that on this side of the ring (our side) we have the Savior, and on that side of the ring (their side) they have the Antichrist, we have begun to co-opt our faith with our politics. We have begun to render unto God what belongs to Caesar and to Caesar what belongs to God.

John Wesley once wrote the following during a heated political season:

> I met those of our society who had votes in the ensuing election, and advised them, 1. To vote, without fee or reward, for the person they judged most worthy: 2. To speak no evil of the person they voted against: and, 3. To take care their spirits were not sharpened against those that voted on the other side.[4]

Yes, John Wesley. Yes.

Here's something else to think about. If I feel more of a kindred solidarity with those who share my politics but not my faith than I feel with those who share my faith but not my politics, what does it say about me? It suggests that I have sold out to Rome. I have rendered to God what belongs to Caesar and to Caesar what belongs to God.

We must recognize that the Bible does not endorse one particular platform over another. Some may argue that their party supports "Christian values" and the other party does not. Both the "Christian left" and the "Christian right" make this claim in every election cycle. But this raises the question, whose Christian values? Which Christian values are we talking about? Are we talking about justice and protection for the unborn? Or are we talking about justice and protection for the poor? The right to hold private property? Or our obligation to care for foreigners and aliens in our midst? Are we promoting the value of an environment in which every able-bodied person has the opportunity and obligation to earn his/her own keep? Or an environment in which just wages, equal pay for equal work, and basic human rights are guaranteed for all people everywhere?

According to the Bible, these are all "Christian" values

derived not only from common sense, but from the sacred Scriptures themselves. It is indisputable that both parties—yes, both—will emphasize some of these biblical ideals but not all of them. It is also indisputable that both parties—yes, both—fail to honor the full range of truth, justice, and freedom that the Scriptures call for in a Kingdom that is truly "from heaven."

To equate left-leaning *or* right-leaning politics with Christianity fails to honor the biblical teaching. Jesus has affirmations as well as sharp critiques for both platforms. As for government itself, God created it. Therefore, government itself is a good and needed thing. Still, the Kingdom of God is not, and was never intended to be, of this world. In this world and for this world, yes; of this world, no.

The point is this. Under Jesus, political loyalties lose their ultimacy. People who disagree with each other politically can also enjoy friendship and common ground as they identify first and foremost as followers of Jesus. Whenever this happens, worldly methods like caricature, spin, and partisan absolutism fade from their politics.

Jesus' Kingdom Is the Only True World-Changing Kingdom

The key to changing the world is not first and foremost having a Republican in power. Neither is it having a Democrat in power. Yes, government is important. God designed it. God often chooses to make good things happen through government, just as he does through business, the arts, health care, academics, the family, and other spheres of influence. When government is at its best, human society enjoys greater flourishing and peace. But government is not, and was never meant to be, the answer to all the world's problems. That's way too much pressure to put on any human or human system. "Seek first the kingdom of God and his righteousness" (Matthew 6:33).

By the third century, in spite of a government that stood against religious freedom, Roman society had been transformed for the better, and Christians played a huge part in this.[5]

Christians led the way in insisting that women share equal dignity with men. They took up the cause of orphans, adopting and caring for unwanted and vulnerable children—"If you don't want your children, please give them to us. We will raise and take care of them," they said to Rome. Among Christians, the sick and the poor were treated with dignity and special honor—including those who were not Christians. Roman society took notice, and within three generations Rome was transformed. People ceased to look to Rome as the ultimate solution to society's problems. Instead, they looked to the followers of Jesus and their radical, everyday, self-donating love. In many ways, Christians found themselves "enjoying the favor of all the people."[6]

The world changes and the Kingdom of God advances as the people of God "season" and penetrate their neighborhoods, communities, places of work, and cities with neighbor-love, with joy in their hearts because Jesus has done the same for them. The world also changes as Christians partner with their non-Christian neighbors, colleagues, and friends in seeking to make the world a better place. Common grace, the good that God brings into the world through all types of people, including many nonbelievers—is one of the greatest gifts God gives to the world. Whether Christian or not, as long as there are people working for the common good, we can (and should) lock arms with them.

In this, we become supporters, not subjects, of our government. This is how God designed it to be. This is the biblical ideal.

Jesus Gains Power by Surrendering Power

Put Barabbas to death and it ends his revolution.

Put Jesus to death and it launches his.[7]

As the crowds panicked and grasped for power, Jesus sat quietly and nondefensively, resolved and ready to die as he awaited his unjust sentence from the Roman state.

Panic and grasping for power is the way of the world.

Remaining calm, loving, and nondefensive, no matter what the political outcomes, is the way of Jesus—and of his followers who have their kingdoms rightly ordered. "Do not fear, little flock, for I am with you," says the King. Do not rejoice when you find yourselves in temporary positions of power and influence, Jesus says, "but rejoice that your names are written in heaven."[8]

Render to Caesar what is Caesar's. Render to God what is God's.

A Way Forward

So then, as we in the United States anticipate the election of a new leader, perhaps we can take a step back and remember a few things.

First, the shoulders of a president are too small to carry a government. Remember that the government is already resting on the shoulders of the Prince of Peace. His Kingdom is already here. Of the increase of his government there will be no end.[9]

Second, the Kingdom of God is above this world and is not of this world. God plays by a different set of rules. His ways are often contrary to ours—and always higher than ours.

Third, Pilate (and, as the case may be, an American president) would have no authority had it not first been given to him by God. The American public will vote as it does because God, in the mystery of his providence, has already cast the deciding vote.[10]

Fourth, the heart of every king and ruler is in the hands of God.[11]

Fifth, believers need to be praying for, honoring, speaking well of, and submitting to their leaders. This is not optional.

If it was true in Rome where religious freedom did not exist, it must be the case in places like ours where religious freedom does exist.[12]

Sixth, let's remember that with very few, if any, exceptions, Christianity has advanced and flourished most when the state was against Christianity, and it has languished and suffered most when the state was for Christianity.

Something to Consider *after* the Election

So then, if you are devastated or irate over the outcome of a presidential election, relax. Things will be okay. We only need, and already have, one Messiah. And he did not lose this election.

If you are ecstatic about an election outcome, relax. Take inventory. We only need, and already have, one Messiah. And he did not win this election.

— o —

SUMMARY: God created government, yet his Kingdom is not of this world. His truth affirms and critiques both right-leaning and left-leaning politics.

SCRIPTURE: Isaiah 9:6; John 18:36
Jesus answered, "My kingdom is not of this world. If my kingdom were of this world, my servants would have been fighting" (John 18:36).

TO CONSIDER: Do you feel that you have more in common with people who share your faith but not your politics, or your politics but not your faith? What does your answer reveal about where your truest loyalties reside? What does it mean that Jesus' Kingdom is *in* this world and *for* this world but is not *of* this world?

Chapter Twenty

BEFRIEND PEOPLE WITH DISABILITIES AND SPECIAL NEEDS

ONE OF THE MOST MEMORABLE SCENES from the movie *Forrest Gump* is when Forrest and Lieutenant Dan are spending the holidays together. In this scene, the lieutenant, who is confined to a wheelchair after getting both of his legs blown off in the Vietnam War, expresses his truest feelings about God. Like many who suffer injury, sickness, or loss, part of Lieutenant Dan's process of finding peace with God includes having an unrestrained shouting match with God. With the unassuming Forrest as his audience, he rants as follows:

> [At the V.A., all they talk about is] Jesus this and Jesus that, have I found Jesus? They even had a priest come and talk to me. He said God is listening. . . . If I accept Jesus into my heart, I would get to walk beside him in the Kingdom of Heaven. Did you hear what I said? WALK beside him in the Kingdom of Heaven! . . . God is listening? What a crock.[1]

Later in the movie, sometime after he and Forrest had gone their separate ways, Lieutenant Dan shows up at Forrest's wedding in a much more settled, restful state of mind. Forrest notices this turning point and later observes, "He never actually said so, but I think he made his peace with God."[2]

Every time I watch *Forrest Gump*, I am most deeply moved when the injured lieutenant is shown to have found peace with God. I am moved because over the years, I have encountered many men, women, and children whose lives have been a magnificent demonstration of the kindness, goodness, faithfulness, and power of God—not in spite of their disabilities, but because of their disabilities.

Heroes in Wheelchairs

According to world-renowned grief expert Elisabeth Kübler-Ross, "The most beautiful people . . . are those who have known defeat, known suffering, known struggle, known loss, and have found their way out of the depths."[3]

I remember pastor Tim Keller saying something similar: the strongest souls are the ones that have emerged out of suffering, and the most massive characters are the ones that have been seared with scars.

One such soul is Joni Eareckson Tada. For more reasons than I am able to count, she has been a hero to Patti and me for years. Joni, the founder of a ministry for people with disabilities called Joni and Friends, has been paralyzed from the neck down since age seventeen due to a diving accident. Joni has also battled stage-three breast cancer. Not unlike Lieutenant Dan, she has endured seasons of wrestling and sorrow and asking, "Why, Lord? Why?" because of her disability and illness. She has wrestled with chronic affliction and has emerged having also "made her peace with God."

Joni wrote the following reflection in response to a question that she, as a Christian, is asked often: *If God is good and if God has the power to do anything, why hasn't God healed you?* To this, she said:

> Those steps [following Jesus] most often lead Christians not to miraculous, divine interventions but directly into the fellowship of suffering. In a way, I've been drawn closer to the Savior, even with this breast cancer. There are things about his character that I wasn't seeing a year ago or even six months ago. That tells me that I'm still growing and being transformed. . . . When people ask about healing, I'm less interested in the physical and more interested in healing my heart. Pray that I get rid of my lazy attitude about God's Word and prayer, of brute pride—set me free from self-centeredness. Those are more important, because Jesus thought they were more important.[4]

On her website, Joni summarizes these same sentiments in a single sentence, where she says, "God will permit what He hates to accomplish that which He loves."[5] How can she say something like this? I suspect that it has to do with her deep awareness of the cross of Jesus, where God permitted what he hates (the violent marring and death of his only begotten Son) to accomplish what he loves (salvation for sinners, whom he loves).

Joni's acceptance of her physical afflictions might trouble us, until we are also given a window into her thoughts about the new heaven and new earth, where, as the Bible says, there will be no more death or mourning or crying or pain. In the new heaven and new earth, Jesus will make all things new, including frail, perishable, mortal, and sometimes disabled human bodies.[6] Reflecting on her wheelchair, Joni said,

> I sure hope I can bring this wheelchair to heaven.
> . . . I hope to bring it and put it in a little corner . . .

then in my new, perfect, glorified body, standing on grateful glorified legs, I'll stand next to my Savior. . . . And I will say, "Jesus, do you see that wheelchair? You were right when you said that in this world we would have trouble, because that thing was a *lot* of trouble. But the weaker I was in that thing, the harder I leaned on you. And the harder I leaned on you, the stronger I discovered you to be. It never would have happened had you not given me the bruising of the blessing of that wheelchair." Then the real ticker-tape parade of praise will begin. And all of earth will join in the party.[7]

When a Wheelchair Becomes a Pulpit

A friend of Joni's named Lynn Wheeler, who was part of our church family here in Nashville, died just a few months ago. Lynn, like Joni, had been confined to a wheelchair for over a decade, paralyzed from the neck down due to a car accident. Before her accident, Lynn ran marathons, played competitive tennis, coached swimming, and played the guitar. She was also a fully engaged church member, friend, neighbor, wife, mother, and grandmother.

While many would grow cynical and angry toward God after such a harsh turn of events, Lynn dropped her anchor into God's promises. I can honestly say that Lynn Wheeler— from her wheelchair—was one of the most joyful, faith-filled, affirming, and others-focused people I have met. Her resolve that God is good in every circumstance, coupled with her optimism about the hope and future that God had prepared for her, led her to speak of her disability not chiefly as an affliction but as her "assignment." Lynn was determined that her disability would be an opportunity for God to receive glory in and through her.

According to Lynn's loving and faithful husband, Doug, when she woke up after being sedated for seven weeks in the ICU and he told her about the accident, the first thought that came to her mind was a verse from Psalm 139: "All the days ordained for me were written in your book before one of them came to be" (verse 16, NIV). Trusting in the faithfulness of God, she would later write:

> My body is a mess right now, but it is well with my
> soul. . . . I know my days are ordained for me, and
> [God] will comfort and strengthen me when I am
> weak. I cling to His truth, though it doesn't make
> sense. His plans for me continue, though everything
> has changed. . . . I take joy in the little things; find
> protection in my limitations. I think of heaven more.

Lynn's favorite hymn, which became the central hymn at her funeral just as it had been the theme song of her life, includes these lyrics:

> *Whate'er my God ordains is right:*
> He is my Friend and Father;
> He suffers naught to do me harm,
> Though many storms may gather,
> Now I may know both joy and woe,
> Some day I shall see clearly
> That He hath loved me dearly.
>
> *Whate'er my God ordains is right:*
> Here shall my stand be taken;
> Though sorrow, need, or death be mine,
> Yet I am not forsaken.
> My Father's care is round me there;

He holds me that I shall not fall:
And so to Him I leave it all.[8]

A runner, tennis player, swimmer, guitarist, singer, friend, grandma, mother, and wife in a wheelchair for the rest of her days after a sudden accident took it all away. And her conclusion to the matter was . . . *I think of heaven more. Whatever my God ordains is right.*

It's no wonder that at Lynn Wheeler's funeral, pastor David Filson declared that in her lifetime, her wheelchair became her pulpit.

Joni, Lynn, and others who draw near to God through their disabilities give me hope for the day when my own mental, emotional, and physical decline arrives. They give me hope that when I am hurting, God will be near, and that as my "outer man" wastes away, my "inner man" will be renewed and made strong. For, just as the apostle Paul said about the disability that he referred to as his "thorn in the flesh," God's grace is sufficient in every circumstance, and his power is made perfect through our weakness.

Indeed, we are fragile jars of clay. We do not lose heart, because in comparison to "the weight of glory" that awaits us in the new heaven and the new earth, even our permanent afflictions are made temporary, and our heaviest burdens are lightened. For the things that we see and experience now—things like diving accidents and car crashes and wheelchairs—are temporary. And the things that we do not yet see or experience—things like renewed bodies and perfect souls and youthfulness that is renewed and will soar like the wings of an eagle—these things are eternal.[9]

It's Not Just the Grown-Ups Who Can Help Us

Speaking of youthfulness and disabilities, did you know that in many cases, people with Down syndrome have a high capacity for enjoying life? Just as Joni Tada and Lynn Wheeler are "preachers of hope" from their wheelchairs, people with Down syndrome can be "preachers of joy."

According to the *American Journal of Medical Genetics*, 99 percent of those living with Down syndrome say that they are happy. Ninety-seven percent say that they like who they are. And 99 percent agree with the statement, "I love my family."[10] According to one writer, these statistics identify those living with Down syndrome as "the happiest people in the world."[11]

One of my greatest privileges is being part of a church with many children and adults who have special needs. Due in large part to the incredible leadership of a woman named Gigi Sanders, our church has chosen to invest resources and special attention into this community. I firmly believe that the greatest beneficiaries of this relationship are not the people among us who have special needs but those of us who get to be in their company.

I think of Katie, who has Down syndrome. She has the biggest smile and gives the longest and strongest hugs. I think of how she lights up when I tell her she is beautiful and how she sweetly reminds me that I need to tell her she is beautiful on those rare occasions when I forget. I think of how she hands me pictures that she has drawn—pictures that represent her profoundly simple yet simply profound interpretations of my sermons.

I think of Cade, who also has Down syndrome. The last time I saw Cade, I was visiting with his parents as he arrived home from a day at school. It was very clear that Cade was a young man on a mission as he stripped off his shirt, located his iPad and earbuds, and headed up the stairs to his bedroom. Within seconds, Cade's voice could be heard all through the house, bellowing his favorite songs by the Wiggles. He sang with gusto and with *zero* signs of insecurity or of self-consciousness.

There was something special about Cade's no-filter, shame-free, man-on-a-mission, bellowing-the-Wiggles approach to life. His demeanor became a fresh reminder to me of how God welcomes and delights in us . . . and in *me*. Rather than a timid, calculated, sophisticated posture in our relating to him, God wants us to come to him "naked and unashamed" through Jesus—with freedom, bold confidence, conviction, and loud singing. Anything less than this represents an amnesia about how deeply, and how recklessly, God loves *us*.

I also think of William, who has Down syndrome and autism. William's parents are stretched fully and are on constant call, working together to care for his needs. And yet they never stop telling us the ways that God reveals himself to them through William. Amid days that can feel like a nonstop, full-court press, William will surprise them in wonderful ways. Not long ago, William got ahold of his father's cell phone and began texting random people on his father's contact list. Each text William sent contained two simple words, and nothing more: *Love you.*

For the remainder of the evening and into the next day, his father received responses to the "Love you" text from family, friends, professional colleagues (awkward!), and also a handful of mild acquaintances (more awkward!). Some responses were affectionate and, as you might imagine, others quite humorous. Each of these exchanges was triggered by a spontaneous, nondiscriminating love note, delivered via the thumbs of a teenage boy with Down syndrome, autism, and an endearingly unique sense of humor.

Sometimes God shows up in the most unexpected ways.

If not for William, people in our church would know Jesus less. If not for William, I, too, would know Jesus less. William wears his ball cap backwards and his sunglasses indoors. He is consistently energetic, often funny, sometimes impulsive, and usually really fast. If you look away for even a minute, he may have disappeared to another room. He laughs at my jokes and gives me high fives, and he smiles ear to ear whenever our eyes make brief contact. William, like Katie, insists on giving me hugs—but in his case, only side hugs that last for a half-second. But he never fails to give me that hug. Maybe it's because William, with full and childlike awareness, *belongs*. And, knowing that he belongs, William has a simple yet deeply profound way of helping others belong too. Though he is unable to clearly articulate his thoughts in words, he hands out bulletins at church, passes the offering plate, and dances happily to hymns and worship songs. As he does all of these things, he brings me back to the truth. He brings me back to grace. William reminds me of the "Love you" that comes to me every moment, and sometimes in the most unexpected ways, from Jesus. He shows me a kind of Kingdom that I would not be able to see without him in my life.

Oh, how we need the Williams and Cades and Katies and Lynns and Jonis of the world to help us see the world, help us see God, and help us see reality through their eyes.

It may be that these beautifully broken friends represent the very perspective that we need in the sometimes-difficult journey of making our peace with God.

Because we are all disabled.

And we all have special needs.

— o —

SUMMARY: People with disabilities and special needs have a unique perspective that can give us hope in the face of our own fears, disappointments, and weaknesses.

SCRIPTURE: 2 Samuel 9:1-13; 2 Corinthians 12:7-10
For the sake of Christ, then, I am content with weaknesses, . . .

hardships, . . . and calamities. For when I am weak, then I am strong (2 Corinthians 12:10).

TO CONSIDER: What disability do you fear or worry about the most for yourself or for someone who is close to you, and why? In what ways have you been touched, personally strengthened, or spiritually motivated by how others have responded to a special need or disability? Why do you think there is so much emphasis in the Bible on how God manifests *his* strength through *our* weaknesses?

Chapter Twenty-One

BEFRIEND THE GOD WHO EMBRACES YOU

IN THE CLASSIC MUSICAL *Fiddler on the Roof,* a husband and wife have two daughters who are falling in love with young men. The husband, noticing how happy the daughters are, turns to his wife and asks her, "Do you love me?"

She responds, "Do I *love* you? . . . For twenty-five years I've washed your clothes, cooked your meals, cleaned your house, given you children, milked your cow. After twenty-five years, why talk about love right now? . . . Do I love him? For twenty-five years I've lived with him, fought with him, starved with him. Twenty-five years my bed is his. If that's not love, what is?"

To which the husband tentatively and nervously replies, "Then you love me?"[1]

Anyone who understands love can see how the wife in this scene is missing the point. For love is complete, love is at its most healthy place, when the *duties* of love are driven by the *delights* of love.

The wife in *Fiddler on the Roof* is in some ways a parable for all of us. Caught up in the pressure of daily responsibilities,

distractions, and the tyranny of the urgent, our most important relationships—the ones that once stirred us and gave us
our deepest joy—become dull and flat. What used to bring us
delight becomes mere duty. What used to stir our affections
becomes an annoyance. What used to be our most tangible
experience of grace becomes poisoned by grudges. What used
to be face-to-face becomes side-to-side at best or back-to-back
at worst. When we prioritize the duties of love and cease nurturing the delights of love, what used to be our greatest source
of companionship becomes our greatest source of loneliness.

It's not just human relationships that experience this erosion
of joy. It can also happen in our relationship with God.

The Martha in Us All

When we lose our intimacy with God, God isn't the one who
has moved away. We are. Consider Jesus' dear friend Martha:

> Now as they went on their way, Jesus entered a village.
> And a woman named Martha welcomed him into her
> house. And she had a sister called Mary, who sat at the
> Lord's feet and listened to his teaching. But Martha
> was distracted with much serving. And she went up
> to him and said, "Lord, do you not care that my sister
> has left me to serve alone? Tell her then to help me."
> But the Lord answered her, "Martha, Martha, you are
> anxious and troubled about many things, but one thing
> is necessary. Mary has chosen the good portion, which
> will not be taken away from her." LUKE 10:38-42

Like the wife in *Fiddler on the Roof*, Martha is emotionally
and relationally impaired because of self-induced performance
fatigue. As she works hard and works alone to serve her and
Mary's guests, her frustration and anxiety are palpable. She is

busy with "much serving," and for this, she has often been criticized. But I don't think Jesus was criticizing her for being busy.

The Greek word Jesus uses for Martha's "serving" is *diakoneo*, a word that is used positively every place it shows up in the Bible. When Jesus describes himself, declaring that he came not to be served but to serve and to give his life as a ransom for many, he uses the word *diakoneo*. When the apostle Paul lays out the qualifications for deacons, a role of help and service in the church, this is the word that he uses also. And when he commends Phoebe as a faithful servant in her local church, he calls her a *diakonon*.[2]

So lest we wrongly dismiss Martha for somehow being untrue to Jesus, we need to give her some credit and grace. Martha is welcoming her guests, practicing the gospel virtue of hospitality. When Jesus addresses her, he says her name twice: "Martha, Martha." The repetition of a person's name in a Semitic language was a term of endearment. Jesus is reaching out to Martha, not scolding her as if she were some sort of rebel. "Martha, Martha" is his gesture of compassion and kindness to Martha, and also to us.

Martha, Martha . . .

. . . before you try to change the world, you must first let me change you.

. . . before you make your mark on others, you must first let me make my mark on you.

. . . before you get busy to make things better, you must first let me make you better.

. . . before you can serve and feed me, you must first let me serve and feed you.

You see, Martha's affliction is not that she is a busybody. Rather, her affliction is that she has a busy heart. She is *distracted* with much serving, and because of this, her very legitimate, life-giving diaconal service is spoiled. She is working from a chaotic center. She is seeking to create order from a cluttered core. She is so busied and distracted by secondary things that she has lost touch with the first thing—which is the *love* that brought her into friendship with Jesus in the first place.

And Jesus longs for us not to lose that love.

> I know your works, your toil . . . I know you are
> enduring patiently and bearing up for my name's sake,
> and you have not grown weary. But I have this against
> you, that you have abandoned the love you had at first.
> Remember therefore from where you have fallen; repent.
>
> REVELATION 2:2-5

These words that Jesus speaks to the church at Ephesus are compelled by the same longing he had for Martha. Jesus *sees* us. He really *sees* us in our striving to be faithful, in our efforts to make a meaningful contribution to his Kingdom. He *sees* how hardworking we can be, how devoted, how enduring, and how faithful we are in our efforts. He *sees* us walking side-by-side with him. But when we walk with him only side-by-side and not face-to-face, it's just a matter of time before we turn ourselves back-to-back with Jesus.

Lord, do you not care . . . ?

Do you hear the heart cry beneath Martha's words? If we listen closely, we will hear that she is after something more than mere relief from her work. What she wants, what she feels she is missing, is recognition. A pat on the back. Affirmation. Approval. Affection. A smile. And she is using her busyness, her productivity, as the path toward getting the recognition.

And the sad thing about it?

The recognition, the pat on the back, the affirmation and approval and affection and smile that Martha is craving and trying to earn through her hard labor is already in her possession. She has forgotten what is already hers.

Drawing Out the Mary in Us

Mary, the sister of Martha, ceases her work when Jesus enters the house. This is actually what separates true hospitality from entertaining. When our mind-set is to entertain our guests, everything must be tidy and just so. But when our aim is hospitality, we will sometimes leave a floor unswept, a pile of dishes uncleaned, and the furniture unarranged. We shift our focus from preparation time to face time.

Mary leaves her serving to sit at Jesus' feet, because her non-negotiable is not her list of tasks and to-dos. Rather, her nonnegotiable is being with Jesus. Among all the things on her plate, among multiple competing options, sitting at Jesus' feet is the "one thing" that Mary will simply not forgo.

Aim first at delight, and you will get duty thrown in.

Aim first at duty, and you will get neither.

> One thing have I asked of the LORD, that will I seek after: that I may dwell in the house of the LORD all the days of my life, to gaze upon the beauty of the LORD and to inquire. . . . You have said, "Seek my face." My heart says to you, "Your face, LORD, do I seek." Hide not your face from me. . . . The LORD will take me in. Teach me your way, O LORD, and lead me on a level path. . . . I believe that I shall look upon the goodness of the LORD in the land of the living!
>
> PSALM 27:4, 8-11, 13

Although it doesn't appear this way to Martha, by sitting at the feet of Jesus, Mary actually becomes *more* productive and *more* equipped to serve with *more* energy, endurance, faithfulness, and passion. We see this in the twelfth chapter of John's Gospel, where we find this same Mary at Jesus' feet again, but this time actively serving him with generosity, worship, and affection—pouring out a pound of perfume that's worth nearly a full year's wages (see John 12:1-8).

Mary's enjoyment of Jesus is precisely what energizes her zeal to serve. For when you are face-to-face with Love himself, you become more loving. When you are face-to-face with Kindness himself, you become more kind. When you are face-to-face with Generosity himself, you become more generous. When you are face-to-face with Hospitality himself, you become more hospitable. It's how Jesus works. He rubs off on us. While Martha is busy trying to be *like* Jesus, Mary spends her energy being *with* him. And in being with him, Mary becomes like him.

Gaining Freedom to Stop and Energy to Love

So then, as one of the hostesses, where did Mary find the freedom to stop and linger instead of doubling down on her busyness? This question is important. Because the answer to this question is also the answer to how *we*, too, can learn to love as Jesus loves.

Like Mary, we gain the freedom to stop and the energy to love by becoming convinced that we are already approved of, already highly esteemed, already cherished and loved and embraced by Jesus, who loved us and gave himself for us.

We often connect Mary more with a touchy-feely faith and less with a faith founded on doctrine. But, it always concerns me when people want to downplay doctrine. "I want a love affair with God, not all this theology," some will say. "I want a faith that *feels* and a love that *does*, so don't give me your doctrine . . . just give me Jesus."

And yet, what did Jesus give to Mary when she sought an encounter with him?

When Mary sat at Jesus' feet, Jesus gave her doctrine.

She sat at his feet and listened . . . to his *teaching*.

You shall love the Lord your God with all your heart and with all your soul and with *all your mind*. This is the great and first commandment.

MATTHEW 22:37-39 (EMPHASIS ADDED)

Do not be conformed to this world, but be transformed by the renewal *of your mind*, that by testing you may discern what is the will of God, what is good and acceptable and perfect.

ROMANS 12:2 (EMPHASIS ADDED)

We destroy arguments and every lofty opinion raised against the knowledge of God, and take *every thought* captive to obey Christ.

2 CORINTHIANS 10:5 (EMPHASIS ADDED)

In our legitimate desire to encounter Jesus, we must pursue the encounter through the avenue of prayer combined with doctrine—the teaching of Jesus, once and for all delivered to the saints, as recorded in the Bible.

Loving God with heart and soul and loving God with our minds are intertwined. They are two sides of the same coin. The way to avoid dead, Pharisaical religion is not to avoid doctrine but rather to pursue a mind shaped by *sound* doctrine or healthy truth.

One of my predecessors at Christ Presbyterian Church, Dr. Charles McGowan, says that doctrine is like the skeleton of our faith. We need the skeleton to hold up and support the rest of the body. But if the skeleton is the only thing visible about the body, it means that the body is either malnourished or dead. The same is true of doctrine. If it's the only thing visible about our Christianity, it means that our Christianity is malnourished or dead.

But for Mary, it was the skeleton of healthy doctrine, of the teaching she got at Jesus' feet, that became her foundation. It was his teaching that provided the basis for the nerve endings and muscles and skin of her faith to move out into the world in strength. For it was at Jesus' feet that Mary learned she was deeply and dearly loved. But she also learned something more.

At Jesus' feet, Mary learned that Jesus *liked* her.

And when you know that you are liked, as Brennan Manning says, it changes everything:

> Tenderness awakens within the security of knowing we are thoroughly and sincerely liked by someone. The mere presence of that special someone . . . brings an inward sigh of relief and a strong sense of feeling safe.[3]

Brennan Manning is echoing Scripture, which tells us that in Christ we are the apple of God's eye, that he takes great delight in us, that he rejoices over us with singing, and that he has similar affection toward us as a bridegroom toward his bride. Nothing in all creation can separate us from his love.[4]

What if we really believed this?

Think with me for a moment. What if we really believed that God, through the generous love and sacrifice of his son, Jesus, deeply *likes* us? What if we really believed that in the sight of God, we have nothing to prove, that being loved is our starting point, that our first and most essential task is to rest in and receive his finished work, that he is quite fond of us and there is nothing we can ever do to change that?

For the Martha in us—that part of us that is plain worn out from trying to prove ourselves to God, to those around us, and to ourselves—what if we started here? What if we started at the place of resting in God's love for us, because he does not stand at a distance from us but welcomes us into his embrace? What if we started by believing that what Jesus says about us is true—that God the Father loves us just as much as he loves God the Son?

If we started here, receiving hospitality from Jesus at *his* table, sitting at his feet and being *with* him . . . over time we might find ourselves becoming *like* him.

May it be so!

— o —

SUMMARY: Energy to serve God and love our neighbor comes not through human effort but by resting in the finished work of Jesus, contemplating his goodness, and receiving his grace and truth.

SCRIPTURE: Psalm 27:4; Galatians 5:1
For freedom Christ has set us free; stand firm therefore, and do not submit again to a yoke of slavery (Galatians 5:1).

TO CONSIDER: Would you identify as a "task" person or a "people" person? How does this impact how you relate to God and others? What do you think about the idea that through Jesus, God loves you and also *likes* you? How would believing this impact how you live?

ABOUT THE AUTHOR

SCOTT SAULS is the author of *Jesus Outside the Lines* and serves as senior pastor of Christ Presbyterian Church in Nashville, Tennessee, where he lives with his wife, Patti, and two daughters, Abby and Ellie. Previously, he was a lead and preaching pastor for Redeemer Presbyterian Church in New York City, where he worked alongside Dr. Timothy Keller. Scott has also planted churches in Kansas City and St. Louis and is a frequent speaker at conferences, leadership retreats, and to university students. He writes weekly on his blog at scottsauls.com.

Connect with Scott online:
Blog: www.scottsauls.com
Twitter: @scottsauls
Instagram: @scottsauls
Facebook: scott.sauls.7
Visit Christ Presbyterian Church in Nashville
www.christpres.org

NOTES

CHAPTER 1: A CASE FOR BEFRIENDING
1. Genesis 2:18.
2. See 1 Samuel 18–20; 2 Samuel 9.
3. C. S. Lewis, *The Four Loves* (New York: Houghton Mifflin Harcourt, 1991), 121.
4. 1 Corinthians 13.

CHAPTER 2: BEFRIEND THE ONE IN THE MIRROR
1. John 3:16; Psalm 17:8; Zephaniah 3:17.

CHAPTER 3: BEFRIEND THE "OTHER"
1. David Brooks, "How to Be Religious in the Public Square," (lecture, The Gathering, 2014).

CHAPTER 4: BEFRIEND PRODIGALS AND PHARISEES
1. Ann Lamott, *Bird by Bird: Some Instructions on Writing and Life* (New York: Anchor Books, 1995), 22.

CHAPTER 5: BEFRIEND THE WRECKED AND THE RESTLESS
1. Thom Rainer, "Pastors and Mental Health," *Thom S. Rainer* (blog), February 26, 2014, http://thomrainer.com/2014/02/pastors-and-mental-health/.

CHAPTER 6: BEFRIEND THE SHAMED AND ASHAMED
1. Scott Sauls, *Jesus Outside the Lines* (Carol Stream, IL: Tyndale, 2015).
2. Jon Ronson, "How One Stupid Tweet Blew Up Justine Sacco's Life," *The New York Times Magazine*, February 12, 2015, http://www.nytimes.com/2015/02/15/magazine/how-one-stupid-tweet-ruined-justine-saccos-life.html.
3. Tim Kreider, "Isn't It Outrageous?," *Opinionator* (blog), July 14, 2009, http://opinionator.blogs.nytimes.com/2009/07/14/isnt-it-outrageous/.
4. Luke 18:9; 7:36-50; John 8:1-11.

5. Brené Brown, "Want to Be Happy? Stop Trying to Be Perfect," *CNN*, 2010, http://www.cnn.com/2010/LIVING/11/01/give.up.perfection/. (Emphasis added.)
6. Matthew 18:15-35.
7. Tim Keller, "How Do You Take Criticism of Your Views?," *The Gospel Coalition*, December 16, 2009, http://www.thegospelcoalition.org/article/how -do-you-take-criticism-of-your-views.
8. Brennan Manning, *Abba's Child* (Colorado Springs, CO: NavPress, 2015), 49.

CHAPTER 7: BEFRIEND THE ONES YOU CAN'T CONTROL
1. P!nk, "Don't Let Me Get Me," *Missundaztood*, 2001.

CHAPTER 8: BEFRIEND TRUE FRIENDS AND SIGNIFICANT OTHERS
1. Arlie Hochschild, "The State of Families, Class and Culture," *New York Times*, October 16, 2009, http://www.nytimes.com/2009/10/18/books/review /Hochschild-t.html?_r=0.
2. See, for example, Ephesians 5:21-33.
3. These qualities are the fruit of the Spirit mentioned in Galatians 5:22-23.
4. Paul Tripp, *Dangerous Calling: Confronting the Unique Challenges of Pastoral Ministry* (Wheaton, IL: Crossway, 2012), 18-19.
5. C. S. Lewis, *Mere Christianity* (New York: HarperCollins, 2001), 110.
6. *A Beautiful Mind*, directed by Ron Howard, Universal Pictures, 2001.
7. Philippians 1:6; 1 John 3:2.

CHAPTER 9: BEFRIEND SEXUAL MINORITIES
1. See Galatians 3:28, for example.
2. Genesis 2:25; Proverbs 5:19; Song of Solomon; 1 Corinthians 7:4-14; Revelation 21:1-5.
3. "Russell Brand Talks Sex, Softcore & Hardcore Porn," YouTube video, 6:27, posted by Fight the New Drug on February 23, 2015, https://www.youtube .com/watch?v=5kvzamjQW9M.
4. Q Ideas, "How the Church Can Change a City," *Q Ideas*, http://qideas.org /articles/how-the-church-can-change-a-city/.
5. Chris Stedman, "Want to Talk to Non-Christians? Six Tips from an Atheist," *Q Ideas*, http://qideas.org/articles/want-to-talk-to-non-christians-six-tips-from -an-atheist/.
6. See Luke 10:25-37; Matthew 9:10; John 4:1-42; Matthew 11:19.
7. Luke 17:11-19; 7:36-50.
8. Madeleine L'Engle, *Walking on Water: Reflections on Faith and Art* (New York: North Point Press, 1995), 122.
9. Matthew 5:14-16.
10. 1 Corinthians 7:8; 2 Samuel 1:26.

CHAPTER 10: BEFRIEND DYSFUNCTIONAL FAMILY MEMBERS
1. Genesis 2:18.
2. John Donne, "Meditation XVII."

3. Psalm 127:3; Matthew 19:14; Ephesians 6:2-3; Matthew 6:9; Luke 13:34; Hebrews 2:10-11.
4. *National Lampoon's Christmas Vacation*, directed by Jeremiah Chechik, Warner Bros., 1989.
5. Luke 4:38-40; Mark 3:20-21; John 19:25-29; Acts 15:13; James 1–5.
6. John 14:6; Matthew 21:31.
7. Hebrews 4:15.
8. D. A. Carson, *Love in Hard Places* (Wheaton, IL: Crossway Books, 2002), 61.
9. Acts 16:11-40.

CHAPTER 11: BEFRIEND THE CHILDREN

1. C. S. Lewis, *The Abolition of Man* (New York: HarperCollins, 2001), 19.
2. Gabe Lyons, "In Defense of Down Syndrome Children . . . Like My Son," *Huffpost Religion*, April 8, 2012, http://www.huffingtonpost.com/gabe-lyons/raising-children-with-down-syndrome_b_1260307.html.

CHAPTER 12: BEFRIEND THOSE GRIEVING AND DYING

1. Steven Curtis Chapman, "Beauty Will Rise," *Beauty Will Rise*, Sparrow Records, 2009.
2. C. S. Lewis, "The Great Divorce," *The Complete C. S. Lewis Signature Classics* (New York: HarperCollins, 2007), 503.
3. J. R. R.Tolkien, *The Return of the King* (New York: Random House, 1986), 246.
4. Blythe Hunt, "Homecoming," *Mundane Faithfulness* (blog), March 22, 2015, http://www.mundanefaithfulness.com/home/2015/3/22/homecoming.

CHAPTER 13: BEFRIEND THE POOR AND EMPTY-HANDED

1. Andrew Revkin, "A New Measure of Well-Being from a Happy Little Kingdom," *New York Times*, October 4, 2005, http://www.nytimes.com/2005/10/04/science/04happ.html?pagewanted=print&_r=0.

CHAPTER 14: BEFRIEND THE OTHER RACE

1. George Yancy, "Dear White America," *Opinionator* (blog), December 24, 2015, http://opinionator.blogs.nytimes.com/2015/12/24/dear-white-america/?emc=edit_ty_20151224&nl=opinion&nlid=54716909&_r=0.
2. Ibid.
3. Clander, "#7 Diversity," *Stuff White People Like* (blog), January 19, 2008, http://stuffwhitepeoplelike.com/2008/01/19/7-diversity/.
4. See the whole story in Acts 6:1-7.

CHAPTER 15: BEFRIEND THE RICH AND POWERFUL

1. Henry David Thoreau, *Walden* (New York: Thomas Y. Crowell & Company, 1910), 8.
2. Madeleine Levine, *The Price of Privilege* (New York: HarperCollins, 2009), Kindle edition.
3. Matthew 25:14-30.

CHAPTER 16: BEFRIEND THE BULLIES AND PERPETRATORS

1. 2 Samuel 11; 12:24-25.
2. Acts 7:54-60; 9:1-19; 13:9.
3. Galatians 1:11–2:2.
4. Sufjan Stevens, "John Wayne Gacy, Jr.," *Sufjan Stevens Invites You to: Come On Feel the Illinoise*, 2005.

CHAPTER 17: BEFRIEND VULNERABLE WOMEN AND HUMANS NOT YET BORN

1. Martin Luther King Jr., "The American Dream" (sermon given at Ebenezer Baptist Church, July 4, 1965).
2. James 2:16.
3. Julian, *Letters* 22, trans. Wilmer C. Wright, Loeb Classical Library 157 (Cambridge, MA: Harvard University Press, 1923).

CHAPTER 18: BEFRIEND STRANGERS AND REFUGEES

1. J. D. Greear, Twitter post by jdgreear, September 5, 2015, https://twitter.com /jdgreear/status/640151179490672640.
2. Chris Rock, *Head of State*, DreamWorks, 2003.
3. The Brilliance, "Brother," *Brother* (Integrity Music, 2015).
4. Luke 4:18.
5. Lauren Boyer, "These Are the 20 Happiest Countries in the World," *U.S. News & World Report*, April 24, 2015, http://www.usnews.com/news/articles/2015/04/24/ world-happiness-report-ranks-worlds-happiest-countries-of-2015.
6. Henry David Thoreau, *Walden* (New York: Thomas Y. Crowell, 1910), 8.

CHAPTER 19: BEFRIEND THOSE WHO VOTE AGAINST YOU

1. Mark 12:13-17.
2. Timothy Keller, *The King's Cross* (London: Hodder & Stoughton, 2013).
3. Romans 13:1-2; 1 Peter 2:13-17.
4. John Wesley, *The Works of Rev. John Wesley, A. M.*, vol. 4 (London: John Mason, 1824), 29.
5. Rodney Starke, *The Rise of Christianity* (New York: Harper, 1996), chapter 5, "The Role of Women in Christian Growth."
6. Acts 2:47, NIV.
7. Keller, *The King's Cross*.
8. See Luke 10:20, 12:32.
9. Isaiah 9:7.
10. John 19:11.
11. Proverbs 21:1.
12. Romans 13:1-7; 1 Peter 2:13-17.

CHAPTER 20: BEFRIEND PEOPLE WITH DISABILITIES AND SPECIAL NEEDS

1. *Forrest Gump*, directed by Robert Zemeckis, Paramount Pictures, 1994.
2. Ibid.
3. Elisabeth Kübler-Ross, *Death: The Final Stage* (New York: Simon & Schuster, 1986), 96.

NOTES

. Sarah Pulliam Bailey, "Joni Eareckson Tada on Something Greater than Healing," *Christianity Today*, October 8, 2010, http://www.christianitytoday.com/ct/2010/october/12.30.html.

5. Joni Eareckson Tada, "God Permits What He Hates," *Joni and Friends*, May 15, 2013, http://www.joniandfriends.org/radio/5-minute/god-permits-what-he-hates1/.

6. Revelation 21:1-5.

7. Joni Eareckson Tada, *Hope . . . the Best of Things* (Wheaton, IL: Crossway Books, 2008), 29.

8. Samuel Rodigast, "Whate'er My God Ordains is Right," 1676.

9. 2 Corinthians 4:7-18, 12:7-10; Isaiah 40:28-31.

10. Brian Skotko, Susan Levine, and Richard Goldstein, "Self-perceptions from people with Down syndrome," *American Journal of Medical Genetics*, vol. 155, Issue 10, October 2011, 2360-2369.

11. John Knight, "The Happiest People in the World," *Desiring God*, March 20, 2015, http://www.desiringgod.org/articles/the-happiest-people-in-the-world.

CHAPTER 21: BEFRIEND THE GOD WHO EMBRACES YOU
1. Jerry Bock, Joseph Stein, and Sheldon Harrick, *Fiddler on the Roof* (New York: Limelight Editions, 1964), 116.

2. Matthew 20:28; 1 Timothy 3:8; Romans 16:1.

3. Brennan Manning, *Abba's Child* (Colorado Springs, CO: NavPress, 2015), 46.

4. Psalm 17:8; Zephaniah 3:17; Isaiah 62:5; Romans 8:38-39.

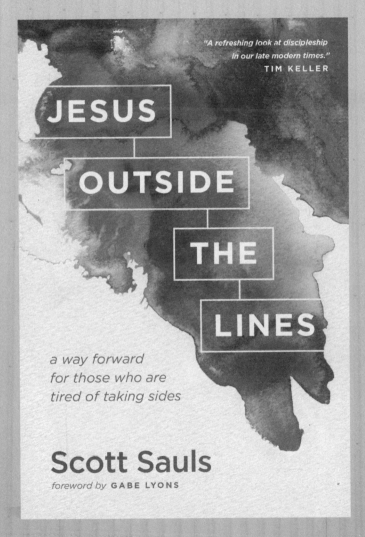

Chapter One

RED STATE OR BLUE STATE?

I met those of our society who had votes in the ensuing election,
and advised them, 1. To vote, without fee or reward, for the
person they judged most worthy: 2. To speak no evil of the
person they voted against: and, 3. To take care their spirits were
not sharpened against those that voted on the other side.

—JOHN WESLEY

SOMETIMES A SERMON CAN BE A POLARIZING THING. Once I was preaching to a crowd of New Yorkers about how Christians should respond to the problem of poverty. I will never forget two e-mails that I received the following week, both in reference to the same sermon. The writer of the first e-mail, among other things, accused me of being a right-wing extremist. The writer of the second e-mail said that he was certain that I must be a left-wing Marxist.

Time for a career change? I hope not.

There are few subjects that cause people to become more heated and opinionated than the subject of politics. Yet in the public discourse, the most heated and opinionated people seem to get nowhere with their heated opinions. During the 2012 presidential election, a friend of mine posted the following on his Facebook page:

Dear person passionately pushing your political agenda on Facebook,

Congratulations! You have convinced me to change
my vote. Thank you for helping me see the light.
Appreciatively yours,
No one.

When I received the two critical e-mails in response to my
sermon about poverty, I shared them with Tim Keller, who at
the time was my boss and mentor. Tim recommended that I
seek to learn what I could from the experience, but not to worry
too much about the negative feedback, because it could actually
be a good sign. For us preachers, Tim said, the longer it takes
people to figure out where we stand on politics, in all likelihood
the more faithfully we are preaching Jesus.

As is the case with every paradox associated with Christianity,
there is a *both/and* and a *neither/nor* component to Christianity
as it relates to political loyalties. Unless a human system is
fully centered on God (no human system is), Jesus will have
things to affirm and things to critique about it. The political
left and the political right are no exception.

That helps me. I hope it will help all of us, especially those
who are tired of the rancor and caricature that so often accompany
political discussions.

The Bible and Government

The first thing I want to say about government is that God
is in favor of it. This should encourage anyone with a career
in public service. Presidents, members of Congress, governors,
mayors, aldermen and alderwomen, as well as police officers,
military personnel, park and school district employees, and
other public servants play an important role in God's plan to
renew the world.

The Bible identifies three institutions that God has established
to resist decay in society and promote its flourishing.

These are the nuclear family, the church, and the government. The focus of this chapter is to consider specifically what the Bible says about government.

We know that Jesus paid taxes and encouraged his disciples to do the same.[1] To those living in Rome, whose government was not always friendly to Christians, the apostle Paul encouraged submission to the governing authorities, who are "ministers of God" and to whom taxes, respect, and honor are owed. Peter likewise tells believers that part of their service to the common good is to fear God and honor the Roman emperor.[2]

> As is the case with every paradox associated with Christianity, there is a *both/and* and a *neither/nor* component to Christianity as it relates to political loyalties.

The Bible also highlights God-fearing men and women who served in public office. Debra served as judge over Israel, Joseph served as prime minister for the Egyptian pharaoh, Daniel served in the court of Nebuchadnezzar's Babylon, and Nehemiah was a trusted official for the Persian king Artaxerxes. Jesus gave high praise to a Roman soldier for his exemplary faith.[3] These and other examples confirm that government, whether in theocratic ancient Israel or secular Egypt, Babylon, Persia, or Rome, has always been part of God's plan.

Whose Side Is Jesus On?

When it comes to politics, the Bible gives us no reason to believe that Jesus would side completely with one political viewpoint over another. Rather, when it comes to kings and kingdoms, *Jesus sides with himself.*

The following encounter between Joshua, an Israelite military commander headed into battle, and the angel of the Lord is instructive:

When Joshua was by Jericho, he lifted up his eyes and
looked, and behold, a man was standing before him with
his drawn sword in his hand. And Joshua went to him and
said to him, "Are you for us, or for our adversaries?" And
he said, "No; but I am the commander of the army of
the LORD. Now I have come." And Joshua fell on his
face to the earth and worshiped and said to him, "What
does my lord say to his servant?" And the commander of
the LORD's army said to Joshua, "Take off your sandals
from your feet, for the place where you are standing is
holy." And Joshua did so.[4]

Lord, are you for us or for our adversaries? "No, I'm not," he
replies.

The question, then, is not whether Jesus is on our side but
whether we are on his. This is the appropriate question not only
for politics and government but also every other concern.

It may surprise us to know that there was political diversity
among Jesus' disciples. Included in the Twelve are Simon, a
Zealot, and Matthew, a tax collector. This is significant because
Zealots worked *against* the government, while tax collectors
worked *for* the government. Interestingly, Matthew the tax
collector emphasizes this diversity more than any of the other
Gospel writers.[5] Despite their opposing viewpoints, Matthew
and Simon were friends, and Matthew wanted us to know this.

Matthew's emphasis on a tax collector and a Zealot living
in community suggests a hierarchy of loyalties, especially for
Christians. Our loyalty to Jesus and his Kingdom must always
exceed our loyalty to an earthly agenda, whether political or otherwise. We should feel "at home" with people who share our faith
but not our politics even more than we do with people who share
our politics but not our faith. If this is not our experience, then
we very well may be rendering to Caesar what belongs to God.

People from varying political persuasions can experience unity under a single, first allegiance to Jesus the King, who on the cross removed and even "killed" the hostility between people on the far left, people on the far right, and people everywhere in between.[6] Wherever the reign of Jesus is felt, differences are embraced and even celebrated as believers move toward one another in unity and peace.

Now let's consider two different ways to look at politics. First, we will consider the world's politics. Then we will look at the politics of God's Kingdom.

The World's Politics

In the eighteenth chapter of John's Gospel, we see a clash between two governors: Pontius Pilate, the governor of Rome, and Jesus Christ, the governor of the universe.[7]

Jesus is brought to Pilate by an angry mob. The mob charges Jesus with being an enemy of the state and a threat to Caesar's preeminence. Pilate, wanting to hear the account directly from Jesus, asks him, "Are you the king of the Jews?" Jesus responds, "You say that I am a king. For this purpose I was born and for this purpose I have come into the world—to bear witness to the truth." Not sensing Jesus to be a threat, Pilate says dismissively to the crowd, "I find no guilt in him."[8] But then he makes a concession according to Jewish custom to release one man for them at the Passover. The crowd pressures Pilate to release Barabbas, a known murderer and insurrectionist, and to crucify Jesus in Barabbas's place. Wanting to please the crowds, Pilate accommodates. Jesus, the innocent man, gets the death penalty. Barabbas, the guilty man, goes free. Modern politics can also work this way.

The goal of politics is to get people to support a particular vision for the world and to conduct their lives according to that vision. In pursuit of this goal, politicians today often use the same strategies that Jesus' accusers and Pilate employed: misuse of power and manipulation of truth.

The Misuse of Power

The world's politics rely heavily on power. Pilate finds himself caught between a rock and a hard place: he believes that Jesus is innocent; he also knows that Barabbas is guilty. Yet the calculating governor is desperate to please the crowds. As he considers the accusations against Jesus, he goes back and forth between his private chamber and then back out to the crowds. Though he knows who is innocent and who is not, he can't decide whom to crucify and whom to set free.

What is happening here? We can assume that Pilate is taking the temperature of the crowd. He is assessing potential outcomes, discerning which course of action will be best for his own approval rating as well as the preservation of his own stature. His conscience makes him reluctant to crucify Jesus, yet he wants the favor of the crowd. But in worldly politics, when conscience and the crowd are at odds with one another, the crowd always wins. When the crowd always wins, bad people can go free and good people suffer.

I love the animated movie *Shrek* for many reasons. There is so much about the human experience that the film gets right. One such example is the pitiful little ruler of the land, Lord Farquaad.

Farquaad is a single man. The one thing he feels is missing from his kingdom is the lovely princess Fiona, who has long been locked up in a castle far away, guarded by a deadly, fire-breathing dragon. There have been many failed attempts to rescue Fiona; many would-be rescuers have lost their lives.

Farquaad gathers his bravest knights together for a competition. The knights are placed inside an arena to duel against each other until only one of them is left standing. The prevailing knight will have the "honor" of going out on Lord Farquaad's behalf to rescue Fiona. Farquaad, himself a coward, offers the following "inspirational" speech to the knights before they turn against each other in the arena:

> Brave knights, you are the best and brightest in all
> the land. Today one of you shall prove himself. That
> champion shall have the honor—no, no—the privilege
> to go forth and rescue the lovely Princess Fiona from
> the fiery keep of the dragon. If for any reason the
> winner is unsuccessful, the first runner-up will take his
> place and so on and so forth. Some of you may die, but
> it's a sacrifice I am willing to make.[9]

The world's politics. *Your* hopes, desires, ambitions, good name—and, if necessary, your life—are worth sacrificing in order to protect and advance *my* agenda. And I will use my power, the authority of my office, to ensure that this happens. *Some of you may die. But it's a sacrifice I am willing to make.* The ends justify the means.

Manipulation of the Truth

The world's politics are also laced with manipulation of the truth, also known as "spin." We see this in the exchange between Pilate and the accusing crowds. When Pilate asks Jesus if he is king of the Jews, Pilate is not interested in spiritual matters. He wants the answer to one question: *Is this man a threat to my power?* Is he an enemy of Caesar, and therefore also my enemy? What is the size of his following? What is his agenda? What kind of momentum is there behind his movement?

Pilate would not be asking any of these questions about Jesus had the crowds not spun Jesus' teaching on the Kingdom of God to mean that Jesus was an enemy of the state. In reality this is a silly and baseless accusation, because Christ's teaching directs his followers to honor those in authority in every way possible. This being true, to the degree that Christians follow the teachings of Jesus, they will actually be perceived as the most *refreshing and cooperative* citizens of any earthly kingdom.

Pilate's agenda was of no concern to Jesus' accusers, because Jesus' growing influence threatened the status quo for them as well. In order to keep Jesus at bay, they created a false narrative about him and went public with it. Eventually it got him killed.

How about us? Are we also prone to exaggerate, spin, and tell half-truths to protect (or usurp) the status quo? How easy it can be to get pulled in to the politics of spin. Some of us have become so used to these tactics and so numb to them that we— yes, even we who claim to be people of truth—have become willing participants in the spin.

On this side of the aisle is our candidate, the answer to all of the world's problems. She can do no wrong. On that side of the aisle is their candidate, the reason for all of the world's problems. He can do no right.

Are such partisan caricatures and political absolutes a Christian practice, or are they decidedly un-Christian? What do you think?

Leaning toward a certain party is one thing (Matthew did it, Simon did it, and Jesus allowed it), but it is important to see that a partisan spirit can actually run against the Spirit of God. If there ever was a partisan crowd in the Bible, it was the crowd that pressured Pilate to crucify Jesus instead of Barabbas. Barabbas, a true criminal, went free while Jesus, an innocent man, was executed after having his impeccable character assassinated. This is the essence of partisanship. Partisans inflate the best features of their party while inflating the worst features, real or contrived, of the other party. They ignore the weaknesses of their own party while dismissing the other party's strengths.

I have good friends on both sides of the political aisle. I

trust them. Many of them—on both sides—have a strong commitment to their faith. Because of this I grow perplexed when Christian men and women willingly participate in spin—ready, willing, and armed to follow the world in telling half-truths to promote their candidates, while telling more half-truths to demonize their opponents. Have we forgotten that a half-truth is the equivalent of a full lie? What's more, political spin is polarizing even within the community of faith.

A Generational Shift

As a pastor I have been struck by what appears to be a strong reaction among the millennial generation (young adults between the ages of eighteen and thirty-five) toward the faith of their baby boomer parents. Some surveys suggest that millennials are either leaving the church or adopting an altogether different expression of Christianity than the one in which they were raised. In an interview with *Rolling Stone* magazine, reporter Brian Hiatt asked Marcus Mumford whether he still considers himself a Christian. Mumford, a pastor's son and a famous millennial (he is lead singer of the band Mumford & Sons), had this to say:

> I don't really like [the word *Christian*]. It comes with so
> much baggage. So, no, I wouldn't call myself a Christian.
> I think the word just conjures up all these religious
> images that I don't really like. I have my personal views
> about the person of Jesus and who he was. . . . I've kind
> of separated myself from the culture of Christianity.[10]

When those who feel a need to distance themselves from Christianity are asked why, Mumford and other millennials cite several reasons. At the top of the list is weariness over the association of right-wing politics with mainstream Christianity. The "culture of Christianity" that Mumford and others want no part of tends to trace directly back to this association. In the realm of politics, millennials have culture-war fatigue.

With this has come a pendulum swing. Wearied by their parents' right-leaning politics, many millennials have shifted toward the political left. There are good things about this phenomenon. Younger, more progressive-minded believers are bringing a renewed zeal for biblical values such as service, care for the poor, inclusion of people on the margins, ethnic and cultural diversity, and other forms of social justice into their communities. What one wonders, however, is how a generational shift to the political left will play out in the long run. Do millennials risk repeating their parents' errors, the only difference being a co-opting of blue-state sensibilities into faith instead of red-state ones? Will their children sense an imbalance in them as well? Only time will tell.

The Politics of God's Kingdom

Please don't hear me saying that it is wrong for a Christian to support one political party over another. Christians have liberty in things that are nonessential, including politics; that's the point I am trying to make here. The political left and the political right both have good things to say, and both have their problems as well. It can be damaging to think otherwise.

For example, during the 1992 presidential elections a friend of mine told me about an awkward moment in his Bible study. One of the group members expressed excitement because that Sunday, she had seen a bumper sticker promoting the "other party" in the church's parking lot. She was excited because, to her, this was an indication that non-Christians had come to visit. Imagine the awkwardness when another member of the group chimed in, "Um . . . that's my bumper sticker that you saw."

Can we talk? If a Zealot and a tax collector share a common faith that transcends opposing political loyalties, then left-leaning and right-leaning believers must do the same. It is wrong to question someone's faith because they don't vote like you do. Yes, *wrong*.

It's Not about Which Side of the Aisle

More recently, a member of our church asked me if I could help him find a Bible study group filled with people he doesn't agree with politically. This really encouraged me, because it shows that there are indeed some Christians who value the growth and sharpening that can come from diversity, including political diversity. This is a man who, unlike those whose maturing process is stunted by blind partisan loyalty, is on a fast track toward greater maturity. As he opens himself to learn from the perspective of others, he also moves toward Jesus, who is neither conservative nor liberal, yet is also both.

> Jesus is neither conservative nor liberal, yet he is also both.

In many ways, Jesus is more conservative than the far right. For instance, he says that "not an iota, not a dot, will pass from the Law until all is accomplished."[11] He warns that anyone who adds to or takes away from the words of his Book will not share in the tree of life or the Holy City. He emphasizes the importance of evangelism and conversion and said that unless you are born again, you cannot see the Kingdom of God.[12] These are all hallmarks of today's conservative Christians.

Jesus is also in many ways more liberal than the far left. In saying repeatedly, "You have heard that it was said . . . But I say to you . . . ," he upends the long-held traditions of his time, establishing a new vision for the world for anyone who would receive it.[13] In this, Jesus is quite subversive with respect to the cultural norms of his time. He says that traditional Jews and modern Gentiles should not separate, but should stay in community together, and that serving the poor is central to his mission.[14] That's all very progressive of him.

How Do We Know We Are on God's Side?

The politics of God's Kingdom are different from the world's politics. Kingdom politics reject the world's methods of misusing power and manipulating the truth. What does it look like for Christians to live out Jesus' Kingdom vision in our daily lives? It looks like taking care of widows and orphans, advocating for the poor, improving economies, paying taxes, honoring those in authority, loving our neighbors, pursuing excellence at work, and blessing those who persecute us. When this happens, kings, presidents, governors, mayors, law enforcement officers, park officials, and other public servants will take notice. Those in authority will begin to see Christians as an asset to society. They will recognize and appreciate that Christians, as citizens first and foremost of God's Kingdom, value leaving the world in better shape than we found it. Consider these words from C. S. Lewis:

> If you read history you will find that the Christians who did the most for the present world were just those who thought most of the next. . . . The conversion of the Roman Empire, the great men who built up the Middle Ages, the English Evangelicals who abolished the Slave Trade, all left their mark on Earth, precisely because their minds were occupied with Heaven. It is since Christians have largely ceased to think of the other world that they have become so ineffective in this.[15]

Let's consider for a moment what history does in fact tell us.

CHRISTIANITY HAS ALWAYS THRIVED MOST AS A LIFE-GIVING MINORITY, NOT A POLITICAL MAJORITY

Some believe that putting Christians in office and other places of power is the key to transforming the world. "If only there were more people in power who followed Jesus," the reasoning goes, "*that* would be the game changer that would finally make the world what God intends it to be." While it is indeed a very good thing for Christians to serve in public office, neither the Bible nor history supports the idea that holding positions of power is *the key* to bringing God's Kingdom to earth as it is in heaven. On this point, Jesus' own resistance to earthly power is telling. At the peak of his popularity, the people wanted him to be king. But he had a different agenda: "Perceiving then that they were about to come and take him by force to make him king, Jesus withdrew again to the mountain by himself."[16]

Why would Jesus resist earthly power? Why would even a "politician" after God's own heart, King David, tell us not to trust in chariots, horses, or princes?[17] Because Christianity always flourishes most as a life-giving minority, not as a powerful majority. It is through subversive, countercultural acts of love, justice, and service for the common good that Christianity has always gained the most ground.

For example, Christians in ancient Rome faced severe opposition and persecution from the state. Yet in this climate, believers had "favor with all the people"[18] because of the refreshing way in which they loved *all* their neighbors. Following many failed attempts to exterminate Christians from Rome, the emperor Julian wrote a letter to his friend Arsacius. In the letter, Julian conceded that the more he tried to destroy Christians, the more their movement grew. Said the emperor, "The impious Galileans [Christians] support not only their own poor but ours as well."[19]

When did Christianity begin to falter in Rome? It began when a later emperor, Constantine, sought to impose Christianity on all of Rome as the state religion. The results were disastrous. Rather than becoming more like the city of God, Rome went into spiritual decline, and the salt of early Christianity eventually lost its savor. The same can be said of many European countries. When those in power made Christianity the state religion, the church began its decline toward irrelevance. More recently, the so-called Moral Majority sought to bring "Christian values" to American society through political activism and "taking a stand" for what they believe. Unfortunately for them, this strategy has had a reverse effect.

CHRISTIANITY EMBRACES BOTH CONSERVATIVE AND PROGRESSIVE VALUES

The Kingdom of Jesus does not advance through spin, political maneuvering, manipulation of power, or "taking a stand" for what we believe (do we ever see Jesus, or for that matter Paul or any of the apostles, taking a stand against secular society or government?). Rather, the Kingdom of Jesus advances through subversive acts of love—acts that flow from conservative *and* progressive values. This is the beauty of the Christian movement. It embraces the very best of both points of view, while pushing back on the flaws, shortcomings, and injustices inherent in both.

How does this work?

By the third century, in spite of a government that stood against religious freedom (except for the freedom to worship Caesar), the social fabric of Rome had been transformed for the better. Believers in Christ were the chief contributors to this transformation. Here are a few examples:

First, Christians led the way in the movement for women's equality. At that time there were double standards in Rome with respect to gender. A woman was expected to be faithful to her husband, while a man could have multiple mistresses and wives. Unmarried and childless women were ostracized. If a woman's husband died, she had two years to find a new husband before the state would withdraw support and she would likely starve. Christians took up the cause of women, giving them prominent places of honor in the church, taking care of widows as if they were family, and insisting that men be faithful to their wives. In spite of prevailing cultural values, a Christian man was expected to be either single or a "one-woman man," the husband of one wife. The virtue of monogamous sexuality within marriage—a conservative value today—was at play. But so was the progressive virtue of equality—men could no longer treat women as inferior.

Second, infanticide was prominent in early Rome. There was no prevailing ethic of life except that certain lives were expendable. Consider this excerpt from a letter by a man named Hilarion to his wife, Alis, who was expecting a child. Hilarion was away on business and sent these instructions about the child in Alis's womb:

> The Kingdom of Jesus advances through subversive acts of love—acts that flow from conservative *and* progressive values.

> Do not worry if when all others return I remain in Alexandria. I beg and beseech of you to take care of the little child, and, as soon as we receive wages, I will send them to you. If—good luck to you!—you have a child, if it is a boy, let it live; if it is a girl, throw it out. You told Aphrodisias to tell me: "Do not forget me." How can I forget you? I beg you therefore not to worry.[20]

It is stunning how upbeat he is toward his wife on the one hand, and how heartless he is toward the child on the other . . . if it is a girl, that is. *"If it is a girl, throw it out."* Sadly, this was all too common in Rome. Christians, however, became known for taking up the cause of orphans (girls, children of other races or with special needs—it didn't matter) by welcoming them into their families and raising them to adulthood. Here we have the conservative virtue of protecting the unborn plus the progressive virtues of championing female equality and social justice.

Third, as in Hitler's Germany, the poor in Rome were coldly viewed as "useless eaters," a drain on society. But in Christian communities the poor were treated with dignity and honor. There was a spirit of compassion and generosity among Christians, which manifested in the sharing of wealth to narrow the income gap—a progressive value. But generosity was voluntary, not forced—a conservative value. I once heard someone say that though the early Christians were monogamous with their bodies, they were promiscuous with their wallets.

My friend Erik Lokkesmoe says that it is the job of Christians to help certain parts of government become unnecessary. Of course he does not mean there should be no government at all, just less need for government in those areas that Scripture entrusts to the church's care. God gave us government to restrain evil and uphold the peace in society. He gave us the church to (among other things) champion the cause of the weak, heal the sick, feed the hungry, and show hospitality to people on the margins. With his statement, Erik calls the church to a renewed vision of being a countercultural movement that works for the good of all.

The Kingdom of God advances on earth as it is in heaven when the people of God, loved and kept by Jesus, assume a public faith that includes, but is certainly not limited to, government. Public faith enriches the world not by grasping for earthly power, but through self-donation. This is how Jesus transformed Jerusalem. This is how Christianity transformed Rome. This is how Christianity can transform any society, including our own.

"Seek first the kingdom of God . . . , and all these things will be added to you."[21]